GO GRAMMAR! 2

A HOMEWORK AND IN-CLASS WORKBOOK

EDITION 4

A COLLINS • M COLLINS • L DERIU • P GARLICK

Punctuation

Phrases, clauses, sentences and paragraphs

Types of writing

INTRODUCTION

The *Go Grammar!* series focuses on the language conventions of English: its grammar, spelling, punctuation, vocabulary and usage. This book uses the metalanguage of English – technical words such as 'preposition', 'clause', 'simile' or 'suffix' – that you need to know in order to discuss the way language is used in your writing, reading and viewing, and your speaking and listening.

This edition of *Go Grammar!* includes the terms and concepts that are covered in the *Australian Curriculum: English*.

Some of the concepts and exercises in this book will be familiar to you. You will be able to work through some sections quickly, revising material that you have encountered. Other sections will be new to you, and you need to be quite sure that you understand each new concept before moving on to the next unit. Ask your teacher to provide exercises for extra practice if you think you need them.

Mastering these units of work will make you a better writer, reader, viewer, speaker and listener. It will also assist you in facing tests such as NAPLAN with more confidence.

Each unit is organised into three sections:

- **EXPLANATION** You will find this box at the beginning of each unit. Sometimes there is a second explanation box later in the unit, to teach you another part of the topic. Memorise these sections.
- **HAVE A GO** exercises: These allow you to practise what you have read and memorised in the explanation. For example, you might need to show that you can identify a part of speech or that you can correctly punctuate.
- **TAKE IT FURTHER** exercises: These exercises are usually more challenging, allowing you to check that you really understand the topic.

You will also find in this book:

- **REVISION TESTS:** Use these to make sure that you have understood the work you have done in the preceding units.
- **SPELLING FOCUS** sections: Use these to consolidate your knowledge of the spelling of English.

Answers to all the exercises in this book are available for your teacher. When there is more than one possible response, we suggest that you work with a partner to check each other's answers. Working with a partner is a good way of making sure that you have understood every topic.

We hope you enjoy working through the exercises in this book and discover new and interesting things about grammar.

AUTHOR ACKNOWLEDGEMENTS

To my children and parents for their kindly light. To Mark, my big brother writer, thank you for your always considerate collaboration.

Adrian Collins

To my family and parents, who see the wood from the trees. To my co-author brother, Adrian, thank you for your good-humoured sense and sensibility.

Mark Collins

Much gratitude to my teaching colleagues and students, and well as the editorial team; as well as Karen, Harry, Nina and Tara.

Laura Deriu

This is dedicated to the many students from whom I have learnt so much over the years, and to Bez, David and James who are so supportive of all my work.

Pam Garlick

Name:

Due date:

Guardian signature:

1 NOUNS

Parts of speech

A **noun** is a naming word. Nouns can be classified as follows:

→ **common** noun – a naming word for a person, place, creature, thing or object	e.g. The *children* watch the *gorillas* at the *zoo*.
→ **proper** noun – a naming word for a particular person, place, thing, business or organisation; proper nouns need capitals	e.g. Many *Australians* fly to *Bali* and *Singapore*.
→ **abstract** noun – a naming word for a quality, idea or feeling	e.g. We discussed the *themes* of *love* and *power* in our class novel.
→ **collective** noun – a naming word for a group or collection of people, animals or objects.	e.g. A child ran from the *crowd* to chase a *gaggle* of geese.

Here is a quick way to check if a word can be used as a noun – see if the word fits in the gap in one of these sentences:

→ (The) ________ is good.

→ (The) ________ are good.

A determiner (the definite article *the*, words such as *this*, *that*, *some*, *any*, and numbers) is sometimes, but not always, used before a noun. The indefinite article (*a* or *an*) can also appear before the noun.

1 Rewrite the following sentences, adding capital letters where they are needed for proper nouns. Circle the eight common nouns.

a The british colonised australia in the late 18th century.

b The first colony was settled in new south wales.

c Janine allis, founder of boost juice, opened her first juice bar in adelaide in 2000.

d Australian students today learn more about indigenous culture and rights than earlier generations.

Noun groups usually consist of a determiner and some adjectives.

2 Draw lines to match the collective noun in the first column with the animal or people in the second column who belong to that group.

a	colony	cattle
b	herd	flowers
c	flock	puppies
d	den	wallabies
e	mob	ants
f	bouquet	directors
g	fleet	birds
h	board	ships
i	litter	thieves

3 In each of the following sentences, there are two nouns. Underline both nouns then circle the one that is an abstract noun.

a Water will satisfy your thirst.

b The soldier was honoured for his courage.

c I loved the humour in this novel.

d They were good friends, but now they have discovered that they are in love.

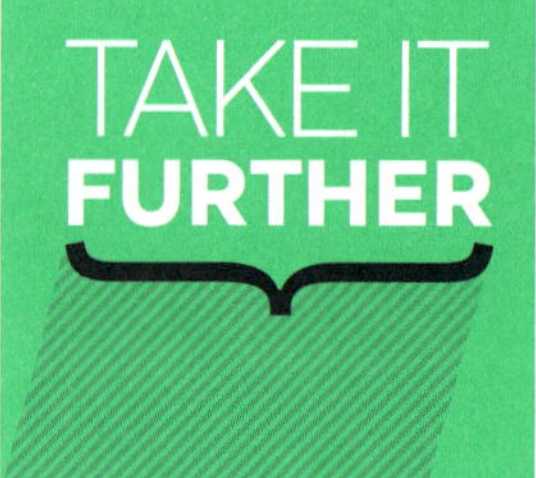

Nouns can also be found in word clusters called **noun groups**: a group of words that builds on a noun and usually consists of a determiner such as *the*, *a* or *this*, plus one or more adjectives and/or adjectival phrases.

The girl in a blue and white sash stood out on stage.

Speakers with a keen sense of social justice and sprightly humour engage students with different interests and backgrounds.

Underline the nouns and noun groups in the following tweets:

a

DoerITau @ DoerITau . 15h
Girls outdo boys in engineering problem solving and take risks in tech problem solving. No surprise or is it? eschoolnews.com/2016/09/26/gir …via @eschoolnews#steamITau #doer #aussieIT

Headline Review Paperback, division of Hodder Headline, London 2006, p. 3

b

A blinder of a game by Sox and Mel hummed in goal attack and the team gelled with a formula one dash out of the blocks after half time. With this great effort, the finals look good.
coachmarigold@sportace.com/2017/07/13

Name: | Due date: | Guardian signature:

2 NOMINALISATION

Parts of speech

Nouns are naming words. The word *nominalisation* comes from the Latin word for *name*. It describes the process of changing other kinds of words, especially verbs, into nouns.

e.g. Koalas in South Australia *were almost exterminated* in the early 20th century.

This sentence can be rewritten as:

e.g. *The virtual extermination* of koalas in South Australia occurred during the early 20th century.

The verb *were exterminated* has been replaced by the noun *extermination*. The focus has moved from the process – the doing – to the deed.

Nominalisation is usually more compact than alternatives and is more likely to be found in formal writing, including academic writing:

e.g. Koalas in South Australia *were almost exterminated* in the early 20th century. They *were widely hunted.*

This sentence can be rewritten, with nominalisation, as:

e.g. *The virtual extermination* of koalas in South Australia was *the result of widespread hunting* during the early 20th century.

Look at these sentences:

e.g. South Australia *has imported* Victorian koalas. This has led to an increase in the number of koalas through breeding, and some habitats have been *defoliated.*

They can be rewritten, with nominalisation, as:

e.g. The *importation* of Victorian koalas into South Australia has led to an increase in the number of koalas through breeding, and *defoliation* of some habitats.

In these pairs of sentences, the first sentences – with the verbs (*imported* and *defoliated*) – are simpler and more direct. The sentences that use nominalisation are denser and more abstract.

Good writers choose the type of writing that suits their readers and purpose.

1 In each of the following pairs of sentences, the second sentence uses nominalisation. The verbs in the first sentence are in italics. Underline the nouns in the second sentences that are examples of nominalisation.

a i Prices for electricity and gas *have increased* considerably and consumers *are asking* questions.

ii Considerable price increases in electricity and gas are raising consumer questions.

b i Scientists *have observed* annual rainfall and *analysed* the results.

ii Observations of annual rainfall have been the subject of analysis.

Nominalisations are more common in formal written language.

c i Candidates *will be selected* based on how they *perform* in interviews.

ii The selection of candidates will be based on their performance in interviews.

d i New procedures *will be established* to *increase* production.

ii The establishment of new procedures will result in an increase in production.

e i Forests *were destroyed* in the recent bushfires. Many animals *lost* their habitats.

ii The destruction of forests in the recent bushfires resulted in a loss of animal habitats.

2 In the following pairs of sentences, the same information is conveyed in two different ways. Within each pair of sentences, you will find one that is more formal and academic. It uses nominalisations in place of verbs. In the space provided after each sentence pair, write whether it is *formal* or *less formal*.

a i Rural and regional Australia expect a faster and more reliable Internet service.

____

ii When we have a faster and more reliable Internet service, rural and regional Australia will be better off. ________________

b i Farmers have known for at least 50 years that their soils are being eroded. They have developed practices to manage this: they now retain much of the native vegetation and they have reduced the number of animals that graze on the land.

____

ii The need to address soil erosion has been evident for at least 50 years. Agricultural management practices include the retention of native vegetation and the reduction of grazing pressure. ________________

c i The advent of urbanisation led to a transformation of Australian lifestyles.

____

ii As more and more people moved to the cities, the way Australians lived changed markedly. ________________

d i The Indonesian invasion of East Timor in 1975 resulted in 25 years of occupation.

____

ii Indonesia invaded East Timor in 1975 and occupied the country for 25 years.

____

In many cases nominalisation involves noun groups, with determiners, adjectives and adjectival phrases.

Underline the keyword or main word in each of these noun groups:

a close observation of animal behaviour

b the recent forest destruction

c Australian community aid in East Timor

d potential suburban development

e significant improvement in Internet speeds

Name:	Due date:	Guardian signature:

3 VERBS

Parts of speech

Most **verbs** are action or doing words, describing physical or mental actions.

 Jane *strolled* to the bus stop.
He *sat* on the fence.

Action verbs can enhance and enliven your writing if you choose adventurously and widely. A precise action verb, such as *strolled*, can create extra meaning and convey a vivid image as effectively as any adjective.

1 Underline the verbs in the following sentences.

- **a** Peter slouched into the principal's office.
- **b** He limped to the finishing line.
- **c** Britain overflows with interesting historical sites.
- **d** The army besieged the castle.
- **e** At daybreak he began his long run.
- **f** The football team triumphed in the face of persistent opposition.
- **g** Jane struggled to the bus stop.

2 The process of replacing verbs with nouns is known as nominalisation (see Unit 2). In the following table, write the noun that can be formed from the verb.

	Verb	Noun
a	agree	
b	conclude	
c	decide	
d	describe	
e	explain	
f	express	

	Verb	Noun
g	inform	
h	invite	
i	persuade	
j	prefer	
k	recognise	
l	reveal	

Action verbs are sometimes called event verbs or happening verbs. There are a few common verbs that are not about action or doing; they are about a **state**, such as being, sensing or relating.

 She *is* a doctor.
He *was* an engineer before he *became* a teacher.
I *feel* excited.
She *seems* thirsty.
He *looks* disappointed.

Vivid verb choices will improve the quality of your writing.

The most common verb in English is the verb *to be*.

 Canberra *is* the capital of Australia.

Public transport *was* an issue in the state election.

Hospital services in country regions *will be* addressed in the budget.

The **verb** *to be* is used to denote being and to demonstrate the existence of a person or thing. It has its own unique forms: *am, is, are, was, were, will be*.

The verb *to be* is often used as an auxiliary (or helper) to the participle of a verb (where the verb ends in *–ing*, such as *running*).

 He *was going* to the museum.

She *is running* away.

Try to minimise use of the auxiliary verbs.

 She runs away.

3 Underline the verb *to be* in the following sentences.

 He is training for the finals.

- **a** They will be at the cinema on Friday.
- **b** The truck was sliding down the slope.
- **c** You are a kind person.
- **d** The tiger is a killing machine.

Use a thesaurus and write five alternatives to these overused verbs.

Overused verb	Action verb alternatives
a go	
b say	
c do	
d make	
e come	
f walk	
g have	

Name: | Due date: | Guardian signature:

REVISION TEST 1

1 Circle the nouns in the advertisement below. Write the correct letter code above each noun: C = common noun, P = proper noun, A = abstract noun, CL = collective noun.

Sylvio and Maria Dino welcome you to this idyllic setting nestled in the Ritch Ranges, a gentle drive for different ages. The atmosphere is stunning. You will see a flock of geese and a mob of wallabies ranging the extensive gardens. Visitors to the exquisite restaurant will savour the rustic cuisine, a perfect conclusion to a local tour or visit to the countryside.

2 In the following table, which uses the language of property development, complete the second column with the noun that can be made from the verb in the first column.

	Verb	Noun
a	construct	
b	develop	
c	observe	
d	agree	
e	compare	
f	decide	
g	conclude	
h	explain	

	Verb	Noun
i	invite	
j	apply	
k	approve	
l	border	
m	protest	
n	beautify	
o	brighten	

3 Many words can be either nouns or verbs, depending on how they are used in a sentence. Write N for *noun* or V for *verb* for each word in italics in the following sentences.

FAIR WORK OMBUDSMAN

Start times and location

→ Checking your start *time* [ ] before your first *shift* [ ] and whether you need to arrive early to complete any paperwork

→ Confirming the address of your workplace, especially if there is more than one site

→ Knowing who to *report* [ ] to when you arrive on your first day

Understanding your duties

→ The importance of checking that you understand what your main duties are

→ Knowing what to do if it's quiet or who to speak to if you have any *questions* [ ] about your job

→ Finding out about, and adhering to, workplace policies around email, social media and personal phone calls

What to wear

→ Knowing the dress code and whether there is a policy about piercings, tattoos or hairstyles

→ *Enquiring* [ ] about whether there's a uniform

→ If there is, checking whether it will be provided or you will be reimbursed for *buying* [ ] it

→ Finding out if there are any safety *rules* [ ] about clothes, shoes or jewellery

What to do if you are sick or running late

→ Knowing who to *contact* [ ] if you are sick or running late

→ Being aware of how to contact that person, i.e. is text or email [ ] ok, or do you need to call

→ Knowing if you're required to provide a medical certificate or statutory declaration if you take sick leave

Fair Work Ombudsman, 'Tips for young workers starting a new job', Media Release, 10 June 2014

4 In each of the following pairs of sentences, the second sentence uses nominalisation. One of the verbs in the first sentence is in italics. Underline the nouns in the second sentences that are examples of nominalisation.

a i The latest figures show that consumers are *losing* confidence.

ii The latest figures show a loss of consumer confidence.

b i All students must *participate* in the athletics carnival.

ii Participation in the athletics carnival is compulsory for all students.

c i Students will be *assessed* at the end of the unit of work.

ii Student assessment will occur at the end of the unit of work.

d i A new science block will be *constructed* to cater for our growing school population.

ii The construction of a new science block will cater for our growing school population.

5 Underline the noun groups in the following work experience advice.

Some professionals downplay their own success ethic with self-mocking jokes, so when you start work experience, exercise discretion and restraint by not playing along if they start criticising themselves – they might think you are attacking them as a newcomer, a telling demonstration of the tall poppy syndrome.

A useful starting point is a smile with attentive listening. This positive approach gives confidence and a team support ethic that professionals expect a young person with enthusiasm and ambition to show willingly and consistently.

Name: | Due date: | Guardian signature:

4 VERB GROUPS

Parts of speech

Verbs show action and they tell us when an action happens – in the past, present or future.

I *watch* the game. (present tense)
You *watched* the game. (past tense)
He *will watch* the game. (future tense)

There are two main forms of a verb:

→ the finite verb (This is a verb that has a subject.)

e.g. He *dances*.
The girl *played* the guitar.

→ the non-finite verb, called the infinitive (You can work out the infinitive by asking what form of the verb goes after the word 'to'.)

e.g. *to go, to hear*

Some tenses are formed using an **auxiliary verb** such as *is, are, was, were, has, have, had, could, will* and *would*. Verbs that have two or more parts, including an auxiliary verb, are called **verb groups** or **compound verbs**. These verb groups often use:

→ the **present participle** – the form of the verb that ends in *–ing* and fits the space: I am ____.

e.g. I am watch*ing* you.

→ the **past participle** – the form of the verb that fits the space: I have ____.

For regular verbs, the past participle is formed by adding *–ed*.

e.g. I have watch*ed* you.

However, there are many irregular verbs in English.

e.g. I have *come*, I have *seen*, I have *done*, I have *lost*.

1 Complete the following table. The first row has been done for you.

	Present	Present participle	Past	Past participle
a	go	going	went	gone
b	stop		stopped	stopped
c	ring	ringing		
d		bending		
e				blown
f		bursting		

Verb groups are usually formed with auxiliary verbs.

	Present	Present participle	Past	Past participle
g			was	
h	catch			
i		reading		
j	am			
k	buy			
l			brought	
m	lead			

Verb groups can be used to form the tense of verbs, showing the time at which an action is happening.

I *am* working *now*. (present time)

I *will* work tomorrow. (future time)

I *was* working yesterday. (past time)

Note that in English there are several different ways of expressing the future.

I *am going* to phone you later.

Tomorrow we work from 9 to 5.

You need to consider the meaning rather than the form of the verb.

2 Write *present*, *past* or *future* in the space after each of the sentences below.

a I expected an answer last week. __________

b I will send you an answer this afternoon. __________

c I like to receive an answer promptly. __________

d I am going to send you an answer this afternoon. __________

e I gave more attention to my homework. __________

f She is proving to be an outstanding musician. __________

g We will help with the Salvation Army Appeal. __________

Participles are not always part of a compound verb.

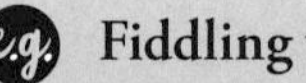
Fiddling with the keys, she struggled to open the door.

When using a participle in this way, you must ensure that it relates clearly to the subject of the sentence.

Quietly waiting in the kennel, she discovered her 'runaway' dog.

('who' was quietly waiting in the kennel: *she* or *dog*?)

This should be written as:

She discovered her 'runaway' dog quietly waiting in the kennel.

Underline the participles in the following sentences.

a Screaming, she ran to the child's rescue.

b He galloped towards the fence, yelling wildly.

c Dodging the opposition players, he kicked the goal.

d They sat outside the principal's office, considering their punishment.

e Battling the strong wind, she guided the ball towards the goal.

f Sweating through his T-shirt, he made it to the finish line.

Name: | Due date: | Guardian signature:

5 MODAL VERBS

Parts of speech

A **modal verb** is an auxiliary verb that expresses a degree of certainty, probability or obligation.

I *might* turn up late for the pizza night. (probability)
I *can* come to the pizza night. (certainty)
I *must* come to the pizza night. (obligation)

Modal verbs include *can, could, must, would, shall, should* and *ought*.

Will can also be a modal verb. Mostly it is used to express the future, but it can also be used to express certainty.

It *will* rain tomorrow. (future)
I *will* get my way, whatever you say! (certainty)

1 Underline the modal verbs in the following sentences.

- **a** Bull terriers can be dangerous.
- **b** Could she come over for dinner?
- **c** When my father was younger, he could run fast.
- **d** I can help you with your maths homework.
- **e** You must leave the dangerous area immediately.
- **f** That might work.
- **g** When you have a broken bone, you must see the doctor.
- **h** They can consistently achieve a high score on the multiple-choice questions.
- **i** With persistence, they might achieve a breakthrough cure.

2 Modal verbs are used to suggest particular shades of meaning. In the sentences below, the modal verbs are in italics. Write *obligation*, *request*, *possibility* or *probability* after each of the sentences, depending on the shade of meaning.

- **a** *May* I go to the library, please, Miss? ________________
- **b** You *ought* to go to the library before school. ________________
- **c** You *must* be present during lessons. ________________
- **d** You *could* go to the library when your work is finished. ________________
- **e** *Would* you like some help? ________________
- **f** You *will* finish this before you leave. ________________
- **g** You *may* go the library at lunch time. ________________
- **h** All library books *must* be returned by the due date. ________________
- **i** I *must* have left my library book at home. ________________
- **j** I *could* have left my library book at home. ________________

Modal verbs allow for fine distinctions in meaning, especially when writing persuasive texts.

The following sentences are in the passive voice. Rewrite them in the active voice.

a He was seen immediately by the doctor.

b The acid was added to the beaker by a careful student.

c The rubbish is collected by the council twice a week.

d A line of trees was planted by the students to form a windbreak.

e The house is haunted by the ghost of the murdered man.

f The children were supervised by a group of parents.

g The balloon was carried away in the wind.

h *Macbeth* and *Hamlet* were written by William Shakespeare.

i The plays were first performed by Shakespeare's theatre company.

j Special theatre venues were built by actors on the outskirts of London.

k Music was performed by a group who sat on the balcony over the stage.

l Cushions were sold by the ticket sellers to patrons who wanted comfortable seats.

m Oranges were bought by theatre patrons as they waited for the performance to begin.

Name: | Due date: | Guardian signature:

7 SUBJECT AND OBJECT

Parts of speech

To find the **subject** of a verb, ask *who?* or *what?* **before** the verb.

e.g. Amman *opened* the bowling attack.

The verb is *opened*. Ask: Who or what *opened? Amman.*

Amman is the subject of the verb *opened*.

e.g. The boys *found* the lost ball.

The verb is *found*. Ask: Who or what *found? The boys.*

The boys is the subject of the verb *found*.

The *lost ball* is the object of the verb *found*.

Find the object by asking *whom?* or *what?* **after** the verb. The **object** of the sentence is the person or thing that receives or is affected by the action of a verb.

e.g. Amman *opened* the bowling attack.

The verb is *opened*. Ask: *Opened* whom or what? *The attack.*

The attack is the object of the verb *opened*.

e.g. The boys *found* the lost ball.

The verb is *found*. Ask: *Found* whom or what? *The lost ball.*

The lost ball is the object of the verb *found*.

The normal word order in English is subject–verb–object. We can usually identify the subject and an object by their position in the sentence.

e.g. Jean likes Mary.
Mary likes Jean.

The subject–verb–object word order allows us to make sense of these two sentences.

1 In the following sentences, use a straight line to underline the subject, use a wavy line to underline the object, and circle the verb.

- **a** The dog grabbed the bone.
- **b** The little dog grabbed the large bone.
- **c** The dog with a studded collar snatched the little dog's bone.
- **d** The crew rescued the sailor.
- **e** The helicopter crew rescued the shipwrecked sailor.
- **f** The girls found the ball.
- **g** The girls from the soccer club have found the lost ball.
- **h** Amman opened the attack.
- **i** Talented cricketer Amman will open the bowling attack.

Remember that a subject must agree with its verb.

2 Each sentence below has three parts: a subject, a verb and an object. Write the appropriate parts of each sentence in the table.

- **a** My best friend Toby likes my sister Laura.
- **b** Eighteen-year-old Marcus used to compete against the girl next door, Aiki.
- **c** Aiki, one of the state's best gymnasts, introduced Laura.
- **d** Aiki now trains with Marcus and Laura.
- **e** Marcus and Laura praised Aiki's performance.
- **f** Aiki achieved a personal best score.

	Subject	Verb	Object
a			
b			
c			
d			
e			
f			

Many verbs in English have both a direct and an indirect object.

e.g. I *gave* the dog a bone.

The verb is *gave*. The subject is *I*. Ask: *Gave* whom or what? The answer is *a bone*.

A bone is the object of the verb. Ask: *Gave a bone* to whom or to what? The answer is *the dog*. *The dog* is the indirect object of the verb.

e.g. I *made* Mum a cup of tea.

The verb is *made*. The subject is *I*. Ask: *Made* whom or what? The answer is *a cup of tea*.

A cup of tea is the object of the verb. Ask: *Made a cup of tea* for whom or for what?

The answer is *Mum*. *Mum* is the indirect object of the verb.

Underline the indirect object in each sentence below.

- **a** My uncle bought John a bike.
- **b** My aunt sent me a present.
- **c** The teacher promised his students a reward.
- **d** I owe my cousin some money.
- **e** The trainer threw the seal some fresh fish.
- **f** I took my father his dinner.
- **g** The committee sent you a letter.
- **h** Students should hand the supervisor their completed papers.
- **i** I sent the coach my congratulations.
- **j** He asked me the time.

Name: | Due date: | Guardian signature:

8 SUBJECT AND PREDICATE

Parts of speech

Sentences are composed of two parts. The part of the sentence that contains the subject of the verb is called the **subject**. The part of the sentence that contains the verb is called the **predicate**. (Remember to include the verb in the predicate.)

The creek | lies at the bottom of the valley.

(subject: The creek; verb: lies; predicate: lies at the bottom of the valley.)

To find the subject, ask *who?* or *what?* **before** the verb. What *lies? The creek* is the subject.

The subject normally comes first in a sentence in English, as in the example above. However, sometimes the order is inverted, as in this example:

At the bottom of the valley lies | the small creek.

(predicate: At the bottom of the valley lies; verb: lies; subject: the small creek.)

1 Circle the subject and underline the predicate in the following sentences.

(Wolves) <u>howl</u>.

- **a** The workers were paid on Friday.
- **b** The wooden house disappeared in the flood.
- **c** The dog loped across the park.
- **d** Which will be replaced?
- **e** We visited the art gallery.
- **f** The energetic goalie broke her stick.
- **g** Mark saw her in the shopping centre.
- **h** Melbourne is now a large city.
- **i** Zoe is in the gym.
- **j** The surfer with the bright blue board paddled vigorously to get over the swell.

2 Underline the predicate in each of the following sentences.

- **a** Bree is a good baseballer.
- **b** We stayed at the island resort.
- **c** I loved the story about the olden days.
- **d** David visited his sick aunt.
- **e** Sarah is a talented debater.
- **f** Year 7 students recited a poem of their choice.
- **g** The distinguished guest speaker spoke of student rights and responsibilities.
- **h** Students like quiet reading time in class.
- **i** They are allowed to choose their own books.
- **j** They frequently recommend books to each other.

In formal writing, sentences usually have a subject and a predicate.

1 In the following sentences, the subject may not be at the beginning of the sentence. Circle the subject and underline the predicate.

- **a** After work each afternoon, George went to the gym before heading home.
- **b** At the beginning of the assembly, the distinguished guest speaker spoke of student rights and responsibilities.
- **c** Across the park loped a stray dog.
- **d** After being sent off, the bad-tempered tennis player broke her racquet.
- **e** Out of the woods came a huge green monster.

2 Fill in the gaps by selecting an appropriate subject or predicate from list below. When you have finished, circle the subject in each completed sentence.

e.g. The orchestra played in the new concert hall.

My university friend

was a distinguished Australian writer.

The intruder

lay at my father's feet.

Year 10 boys

Overseas workers

might be possible after further investigation of Mars.

Melbourne Storm

practised their lay-ups at training.

was diverted to Singapore airport.

Our swimming team

like the council's skateboarding facility.

- **a** ______________________ will play in Saturday's rugby league match.
- **b** Young skateboarders ______________________.
- **c** ______________________ was apprehended by the police.
- **d** The dog with the curly coat ______________________.
- **e** ______________________ often read sports biographies.
- **f** ______________________ achieved a silver medal in the Olympics.
- **g** The plane ______________________.
- **h** ______________________ worked part-time at a fast-food restaurant.
- **i** The basketball team ______________________.
- **j** Martin Boyd ______________________.
- **k** ______________________ will be contracted to work in Western Australia.
- **l** Space travel ______________________
______________________.

Name: | Due date: | Guardian signature:

REVISION TEST 2

1 Underline the verbs in the following sentences.

a Peter played at the sports ground.

b I sang in the concert.

c A swarm of wasps attacked the gardener.

d She hikes in the mountain range with a group of friends.

e Emma likes the gym.

f After the storm the sun will shine.

g The kangaroo leapt from the rocks.

h During the play the audience hooted with laughter.

i The tall ships were sailing up the harbour.

j That outfit cost little.

2 Complete the following sentences by adding both the past and future forms of the verbs in the brackets.

a Jack ________________/__________________ the siren. (to ring)

b The farmer ________________/__________________ the sheep. (to shear)

c Simon ________________/__________________ the parcel on the table. (to lay)

d Kate ________________/__________________ on the beach. (to lie)

e I ________________/__________________ my horse in the paddock. (to ride)

f Marco ________________/__________________ work at eight o'clock. (to begin)

g The dinghy ________________/__________________ in the lake. (to sink)

h We ________________/__________________ the house on the hill. (to build)

i He ________________/__________________ to the people at the kennels. (to speak)

j The fire ________________/__________________ brightly. (to burn)

3 Some of the sentences below have a basic subject–verb structure and some have a subject–verb–object structure. Write *S–V* or *S–V–O* after each sentence.

a The bird sings sweetly. ________________

b The choir sang a folk song. ________________

c The music was loud. ________________

d The showband played some swing music. ________________

e The audience lingered after the performance. ________________

f The audience applauded the orchestra. ________________

4 The following sentences are in the passive voice. Rewrite them in the active voice.

a The recruits were addressed by a senior officer.

b A try was scored by the rugby star.

c Your assignment will be collected by your class teacher at the end of the week.

d A pride of lions was watched by tourists.

e The sonata was played by an eminent pianist.

f A community aid project was sponsored by our class.

g Peace is desired by many people.

h The comprehension section was rushed by some students.

i The results of the first essay were used by our teacher to revise sentence structure.

j A child's personal development and knowledge of a subject are seen by parents as important priorities.

5 Underline the indirect object in each of the following sentences.

a He made me a birthday cake.

b The teacher gave him his assignment.

c Dad gave my sister a new bike.

d He baked chocolate cookies for me.

Name: | Due date: | Guardian signature:

9 PERSONAL PRONOUNS

Parts of speech

A **pronoun** is a word used in place of a noun (*pro* means 'for' the noun).
A personal pronoun is used in place of a noun that names people, animals or objects.

e.g. *They* told *me* I can improve *it*.

We usually label personal pronouns according to:

→ **person** (first person is the person speaking, second person is the person being spoken to and third person is the person or thing being spoken about)
→ **gender** (male, female or thing)
→ **number** (singular or plural).

	Singular (one)		Plural (more than one)	
	Subject	Object	Subject	Object
First person	I	me	we	us
Second person	you	you	you	you
Third person	he/she/it	him/her/it	they	them

1 Write the correct form of the personal pronoun in each of the following sentences.

- **a** My brother reimbursed ________________ for the money I gave him.
- **b** My dad gave me two book vouchers and I gave one of ________________ to my sister.
- **c** Will ________________ improve their performance?
- **d** If ________________ cannot stand the heat, then you better get out of the kitchen!
- **e** Please drop ________________ in the box on your way out.
- **f** The ergonomist told ________________ all to keep our backs straight when seated.
- **g** ________________ all decided that it was time for us to go home.
- **h** If it had been me, ________________ would have reacted differently.
- **i** Rachel asked ________________ parents to pick her up after the formal.

2 Underline the personal pronouns in the following student review of cycling.

> I started cycling to lose some weight and increase my fitness. It is comfortable wearing Lycra and I love having the company of my best friend, Sophie. She told me cycling boosts vitamin D levels and helps us feel good. We enjoy weekends much more now.

The form of most pronouns changes depending on whether it is in the *subject* or *object* position. You need to check that you have the correct form.

3 Underline the pronouns in the following letter to the editor. Write the person and number for each different pronoun in the space below.

Our water is precious. If we use it wisely, we have more to share and could be free of water restrictions. If we conserve water, then we will have enough water for gardens, birds and animals. If we hose the driveway, it just goes down the drain and for no common good. Water-saving devices in homes, gardens, schools and council properties are recommended. They contribute to the community goal of saving more water for better use. You can do your bit.

Writers choose the voice in which the story will be told. Sometimes a writer will pretend to be one of the characters and will tell the story in the *first person*: 'I did this' and 'I said that'. First-person narration is an effective way to involve your readers but the narrator's view of the world is limited to what he or she experiences. A first-person narrator may also be unreliable. He or she may not understand what they are relating, or there may be a deliberate attempt to mislead the reader.

Many stories are told by an unidentified narrator who knows everything and can tell us what all the characters are thinking and feeling. This narrative voice is called the *omniscient* or *all-knowing* narrator, who uses the third person: 'he said', 'she did', 'they thought'.

Stories are very rarely told in the second person (*you*) and only sometimes in the third-person plural (*we*). Think carefully: is it better for me to write in the first or third person?

Change the following sentences into third-person narrative.

a I saw, I came, I conquered.

b You all know that honesty is the best policy.

c My father said I should put in more effort.

d It is your responsibility to put the rubbish in the wheelie bin.

e It is our responsibility to work as a team and play to our best.

Name: | Due date: | Guardian signature:

10 ADJECTIVES

Parts of speech

An **adjective** adds to the meaning of a noun or pronoun. When talking grammatically, we say an adjective *qualifies* a noun or pronoun.

e.g. She wore a *tiny* hat.

The adjective *tiny* qualifies the noun *hat*.

e.g. We met some *entertaining* sailors.

The adjective *entertaining* qualifies the noun *sailors*.

1 Select suitable adjectives to go with the following nouns. Swap your work with a partner's and check each other's answers, making sure you have used adjectives.

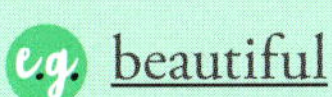

e.g. beautiful baby

a ________________ wolf
b ________________ house
c ________________ yacht
d ________________ Earth
e ________________ castle
f ________________ bush
g ________________ surfer
h ________________ storm
i ________________ paddocks

2 Underline the adjectives and circle the nouns they qualify.

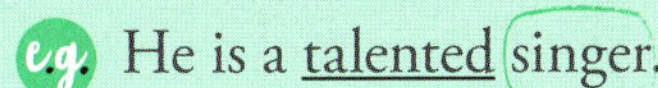

e.g. He is a talented singer.

a He was a courageous soldier.
b The nurse was helpful.
c The dawn was beautiful.
d She was in terrible agony.
e The tiny seahorse attached itself to the floating seaweed.
f It was a magnificent horse.
g The church bell rang out clearly that summer morning.
h Marina is a lively young girl.

Choose the adjective with the precise shade of meaning that you need in your writing. Use your dictionary for a choice of adjectives.

3 In the passage below, you can see how the adjectives work to describe the nouns. List each adjective and then record who or what it describes.

> Papa, as the little children called him, was old and bent. His tiny, one-roomed house was hidden behind the thick, green hedge, which surrounded the paved schoolyard. He had a happy smile and an encouraging word for the children.

TAKE IT FURTHER

1 An antonym is a word *opposite* in meaning to another word (see Unit 20). Write antonyms for these adjectives. Do not use the prefixes *un-* or *in-*.

e.g. shallow – deep

	Adjective	Antonym
a	inferior	
b	wise	
c	false	
d	mean	
e	happy	
f	proud	

	Adjective	Antonym
g	smooth	
h	wild	
i	empty	
j	dark	
k	easy	
l	shiny	

2 Change these nouns into adjectives.

e.g. pride – proud

	Noun	Adjective
a	innocence	
b	wool	
c	value	
d	courtesy	
e	disaster	
f	danger	

	Noun	Adjective
g	doubt	
h	sorrow	
i	suspicion	
j	weariness	
k	falsehood	
l	defiance	

Name: | Due date: | Guardian signature:

11 ADVERBS

Parts of speech

An **adverb** modifies a verb, an adjective or another adverb, adding meaning. Used with a verb, an adverb tells us how (manner), when (time), where (place) and to what extent (degree) something happened.

The boy ran *slowly*. (manner)
We will go *shortly*. (time)
She searched *everywhere*. (place)
The room is *too* hot. (degree)

Many adverbs can be formed by adding –ly to an adjective, but there are often changes to the spelling.

→ For words ending in *–l*, double the *l*:

e.g. *respectful – respectfully; joyful – joyfully*

→ For words ending in *–y*, you usually change the *y* to *i* before adding *–ly*.

e.g. *angry – angrily; dreamy – dreamily* (exception: *dry – dryly*)

Note: this rule does not apply if the letter before the –y is a vowel:

e.g. *gay – gaily; day – daily*

→ For words ending in *–e*, you may need to drop the *e* before adding *–ly*

e.g. *visible – visibly; tangible – tangibly* (exceptions: *extreme – extremely; distinctive – distinctively*)

Note: this rule only applies to words of more than one syllable.

free – freely

1 Add appropriate adverbs to complete the following sentences.

The thief ran <u>away</u> from the police.

a The skier shrieked ____________________ as she headed towards the cliff.

b The children laughed ____________________ at the puppet show.

c The truck was driven ____________________ down the gravel road.

d Smoke curled ____________________ from the camp fire.

e The hang-glider spiralled ____________________ to the ground.

2 Underline the five adverbs in the following paragraph from a newspaper article.

The vast majority of packed pre-schoolers' lunches are stored unsafely, a US study discovered recently. Researchers testing perishable food brought by kids to a group of childcare centres in Texas found more than 97 per cent of meats, dairy and vegies were too warm. The NSW Food Authority strongly advises parents to use insulated lunchboxes and regularly pack a frozen bottle or freezer brick next to perishable food.

Adverbs of degree such as *very*, *quite* or *too* usually modify adjectives or other adverbs. Minimise their use in your writing.

3 Form adverbs from the following adjectives. Take care with the spelling.

	Adjective	Adverb		Adjective	Adverb
a	careful		**i**	immediate	
b	free		**j**	solemn	
c	severe		**k**	quick	
d	satisfactory		**l**	angry	
e	changeable		**m**	critical	
f	drowsy		**n**	laughable	
g	peaceful		**o**	confident	
h	protective		**p**	professional	

4 In the table below, arrange the following adverbs into three groups according to their spelling then write a statement for each group explaining what happens when you add *-ly* to form an adverb.

admirably	doubtfully	frostily	preferably	terribly
angrily	equally	happily	really	thoughtfully
beautifully	fashionably	horribly	satisfactorily	wearily

Group 1	Group 2	Group 3

TAKE IT FURTHER

Adverbs that do not have the –ly suffix include:

→ time – such as *soon, yesterday, today, tomorrow, later*

→ place – such as *there, everywhere, somewhere*

→ degree – such as *most, quite, rather, too, very*.

Complete each sentence below with a suitable adverb from the list above.

a He was a ________________ talkative child. (degree)

b They took the money to the bank ________________. (time)

c The book was ________________ in the room. (place)

d I'm expecting him to arrive ________________, probably at any moment. (time)

e This new fashion seems to have been picked up ________________. (place)

f I am ________________ sure that I've already seen that film. (degree)

Name: | Due date: | Guardian signature:

12 COMPARISON OF ADJECTIVES AND ADVERBS

Parts of speech

An **adjective** is a word that describes a noun or pronoun and adds meaning to that noun or pronoun. Adjectives may also be used to compare nouns or pronouns.

e.g. This is a *big* house.

This is called the **positive** form of the adjective.

e.g. This is a *bigger* house.

This is called the **comparative** form of the adjective. It is used for comparing two things.

e.g. This is the *biggest* house.

This is called the **superlative** form of the adjective. It is used for comparing three or more things.

Note that if the adjective is a small word (two syllables or fewer) or ends in –y, you can simply add *–er* (comparative) or *–est* (superlative). If the word is longer, then you form the comparative or superlative by placing *more* or *most* before the adjective.

e.g. big, bigg*er*, bigg*est*; happy, happ*ier*, happ*iest*; beautiful, *more* beautiful, *most* beautiful

Regular comparisons		
Positive	**Comparative**	**Superlative**
small	smaller	smallest
delightful	more delightful	most delightful
Irregular comparisons		
Positive	**Comparative**	**Superlative**
bad	worse	worst
little (volume)	less	least
little (size)	littler	littlest
old	older/elder	oldest/eldest
many	more	most

1 Complete the following sentences using the comparative form of the adjective in brackets.

a She was the ____________________ of the two children. (sweet)

b We were ____________________ than the others. (late)

c I had never seen ______________________country. (mountainous)

Be careful not to overuse the superlative form of adjectives and adverbs.

4 Write the comparative and superlative forms of the adjectives.

Positive	Comparative	Superlative
a beautiful		
b lengthy		
c sad		
d good		
e bad		
f old		
g ugly		
h tedious		
i costly		

5 Write the adjectives and adverbs of these word families.

Noun	Adjective	Adverb
a arrogance		
b happiness		
c generosity		
d satisfaction		
e intelligence		
f selection		
g sympathy		
h enjoyment		
i disappointment		
j prosperity		
k functionality		

6 Fill in the gap in each adverb with the missing letter.

a angr__ly

b satisfactor__ly

c happ__ly

d wear__ly

e thirst__ly

f drows__ly

g frost__ly

h blood__ly

i hatefu__ly

j resentfu__ly

k playfu__ly

l mournfu__ly

Name: | Due date: | Guardian signature:

13 PREPOSITIONS

Parts of speech

A **preposition** shows the relationship between people, things and actions. Common prepositions include:

about	at	during	inside	out	under
across	below	except	near	outside	with
after	beneath	for	of	over	without
against	between	from	on	to	
among	by	in	onto	towards	

e.g. Claudio's car was parked *below* the building.
The skateboard park is *behind* the tram depot.
Moira stayed at the party *until* midnight.

1 Underline the preposition(s) in the sentences below.

- **a** We hiked over hills and valleys.
- **b** The girls rowed in fours.
- **c** I stared at the strange picture.
- **d** The singer performed by night and slept during the day.
- **e** The warlock appeared in a black coat and boots.
- **f** The gang gathered inside the garage where they could not be seen.
- **g** The class complained about the lack of ventilation in summer.

2 Write appropriate prepositions in the following sentences. Use the prepositions listed above.

- **a** ____________ dawn three rabbits scurried ____________ the paddock.
- **b** ____________ the bridge we noticed a beautiful flower garden.
- **c** The teacher sat ____________ two disruptive students ____________ school assembly.
- **d** ____________ the rain, the villagers came ____________ to resume their cricket match ____________ the clearing.
- **e** We were pushed ____________ the security fence ____________ the stage.
- **f** Wayne cleared out the garage ____________ order to make space ____________ his motorbike.
- **g** Tracey backed away ____________ the ferocious dog growling ____________ her.
- **h** Given the state ____________ the world today, nearly everyone would say that we need to do more ____________ the environment.
- **i** All of these boxes ____________ the one ____________ the door can be taken to the rubbish tip.

Some words are always followed by the same preposition, such as *sympathise with* or *rely on*.

3 Complete the passage with the appropriate prepositions from the list below.

beneath	into	in	at
behind	towards	out of	of

I moved ______ the shriek as if I were ______ a dream. I turned the handle ______ the door and, ______ fear, jumped well ______ the dark room to avoid being hit by someone ______ the door. Then I saw a figure crouching ______ a table and I knew that I had arrived ______ the destination of my quest.

4 **Underline the ten prepositions in the following advice about how to bat in cricket.**

When you arrive at the crease, keep it simple. Look briefly at the positions of the fielders around you. Stand comfortably with your bat placed between your feet. Don't tighten your grip on the bat handle. Relax and flex your feet. At the moment the bowler releases the ball, move your feet and bat with your eyes steady on the ball to where you think you can meet the pitched ball.

5 **Some prepositions are always used after certain verbs or adjectives. Fill in the missing prepositions in the sentences below.**

a His score in the exam has shown that he is capable ______ succeeding.
b She shouldn't depend ______ last-minute cramming for the test.
c He has been encouraged ______ his results.
d She was driven ______ her mother.
e He was surprised ______ his success.
f I'm still not completely satisfied ______ her attitude.
g I'm accustomed ______ students who are prepared to work harder.
h I am nevertheless thankful ______ his progress.

TAKE IT FURTHER

When a pronoun is used after a preposition, it is in the *object* position, so you must use the object form.

e.g. There is a close understanding between the President and me.

Underline the correct form of the pronoun from the options in brackets.

a I have some books for (he/him) and (she/her).
b This is a secret between you and (we/us).
c The question will be settled between Maria and (I/me).
d I used to live near (they/them).
e They used to live next to (we/us).
f There is no difference of opinion between my party and (I/me).
g Faults and disappointments do not deter my best friend and (I/me) trusting each other.
h My mother and (I/me) have a 'no mobile' rule when we sit down to talk at dinner.
i The beauty of the sunset left dad and (I/me) speechless for a while.

Name: | Due date: | Guardian signature:

14 CONJUNCTIONS

Parts of speech

Conjunctions are joining words, used to connect words, phrases and clauses.

e.g. My favourite fruits are peaches *and* strawberries.
He walked down the stairs *and* out the front door.
I read the whole book in one session *because* I wanted to know the ending.

Coordinating conjunctions join words and phrases that have equal status. They also join main (or independent) clauses. They include *and*, *but*, *or*, *nor*, *yet*.

e.g. Do you want flake *or* whiting?
I love playing tennis *and* watching the Australian Open on TV.
The workers went on strike *but* returned to work after they gained better conditions.

Subordinating conjunctions join subordinate (or dependent) clauses to main clauses. Subordinate conjunctions include:

after	as	before	where
although	because	since	while

e.g. Collingwood competed desperately throughout the match (main clause) *although* the team suffered injuries. (subordinate clause)

Because some players have injuries, (subordinate clause) we will need to field some inexperienced players next week. (main clause)

1 Join each pair of the sentences to make one sentence, using the conjunction in brackets.

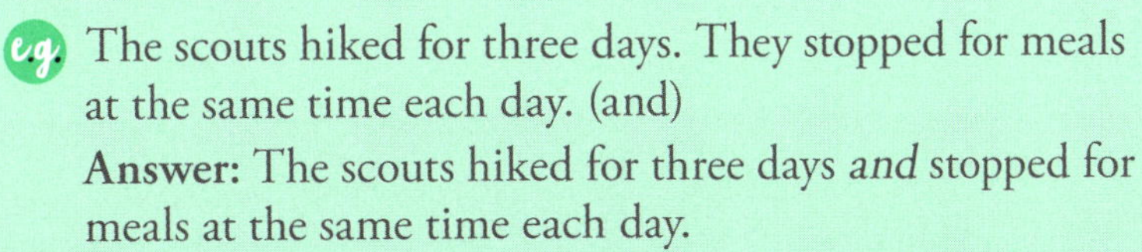

e.g. The scouts hiked for three days. They stopped for meals at the same time each day. (and)
Answer: The scouts hiked for three days *and* stopped for meals at the same time each day.

a My parents spoke to me. They had had an interview with my teacher. (after)

b I am the better dancer. The other girl is very talented. (although)

c You should go outside to play. You are not needed in the kitchen. (because)

Improve your writing by using conjunctions to join sentences.

d My brother is chopping the tomatoes. His friend is putting the pasta on to boil. (while)

e The neighbour stood at the mailbox. He waited for the post van. (and)

f The farmer stood at the gate. A stray cow wandered by. (as)

g The dancer stood on the stage. He did not wait for the orchestra to begin. (but)

2 Change the following group of simple sentences into a paragraph containing four sentences. You will need to use conjunctions. There are several ways of doing this. You could swap your work with a partner's and check each other's answers.

The fighter jet was on fire. It roared over the airfield. There was nothing the ground crew could do. The multimillion-dollar plane banked into a dive. The residential area lay just ahead. Onlookers waited for the worst. A huge explosion was heard on the vacant playing field. A white parachute could barely be seen floating above the wreckage.

TAKE IT FURTHER

Look at the three examples below. Which do you think reads best? Give a reason for your answer.

a I don't like watching films about vampires. The reason I don't like watching them is that they are frightening. I don't like watching them when I am alone at night.

b I don't like watching films about vampires and the reason I don't like watching them is that they are frightening and I don't like watching them when I am alone at night.

c When I am alone at night, I don't like watching films about vampires because they are frightening.

Name: Due date: Guardian signature:

Parts of speech

REVISION TEST 4

1 Underline the prepositions in the following sentences.

a She rode through the desert on a horse with no name.

b They sang the anthem before and after the game.

c The nurse received awards both for his bravery during the war and for his community service after it.

d She will be waiting opposite the bank until three o'clock.

e Neither boy spoke to me.

f The police officer fell against her car but managed to keep on her feet.

g In rural communities, people are often kind to visitors.

2 Underline the conjunctions, including subordinating conjunctions, in the following passage.

After the snow fell, people were happy. People played in the snow before they had breakfast. A toddler and her parents built a snowman but they soon left for other distractions. Both the ski lift and cable car operated without problems. Large queues of skiers waited patiently before they could buy tickets for the ski lift. Others took the cable car to the peak where the view was magnificent.

3 Some words can be used as either prepositions or conjunctions, depending on their function in the sentence. In the following pairs of sentences, decide whether the italicised word is used as a preposition or a conjunction. Write *preposition* or *conjunction* after each sentence.

a i You need to finish your homework *before* you watch television. ________________

ii You need to finish your chores *before* tea. ________________

b i *After* the bell rang, we strolled to the bus stop. ________________

ii *After* the last lesson, we ran to the lockers. ________________

c i *Until* now I hadn't decided what to do. ________________

ii *Until* I heard your explanation, I hadn't considered another option. ________________

d i *As* a parent, I understand your concern. ________________

ii *As* I am now a parent, I understand your concern. ________________

e i *Before* you go out to recess, you need to finish those problems. ________________

ii *Before* recess, you need to finish those problems. ________________

f i *Since* the party I have changed my mind about her. ________________

ii *Since* I saw the way she behaved at the party, I have liked her. ________________

g i *As* members of the team, you are expected to work together. ________________

ii *As* you are all members of the team, you are expected to work together. ________________

4 Conjunctions can be used to join words, phrases or clauses. Underline the conjunctions in the following sentences and write *word*, *phrase* or *clause* after each sentence.

a My teacher is demanding but kind. ______________

b The stolen car screamed around the corner and down our street. ______________

c The plane circled the airport and then landed on the runway. ______________

d Hands and throat tight, I braced for the collision. ______________

e When I heard the choir sing, I felt lifted. ______________

f Fruit is nutritious but expensive. ______________

g Fruit is nutritious but it can be expensive out of season. ______________

h My favourite sports are sailing and soccer. ______________

i My favourite sports are watching tennis and cricket. ______________

j I like playing tennis and I also like umpiring cricket. ______________

5 Two sentences can be joined by a conjunction to make a new sentence. There are different ways to combine sentences, depending on where you want to place the emphasis in the new sentence. Join the two sentences in the box below following the instructions.

> We finished the test.
>
> The recess bell sounded.

a Make the first sentence the main idea. Join the second sentence to the first sentence with the conjunction *as*.

____

b Make the second sentence the main idea. Join the first sentence to the second sentence with the conjunction *as*.

____

c Make the first sentence the main idea. Use the conjunction *after*.

____

d Make the second sentence the main idea. Use the conjunction *after*.

____

e Make the first sentence the main idea. Use the conjunction *before*.

____

f Make the second sentence the main idea. Use the conjunction *before*.

____

Name: | Due date: | Guardian signature:

Parts of speech

SPELLING FOCUS 1

English spelling has many irregularities, but there are useful spelling rules.

- → The rule for one-syllable words when adding *-ing* or *-ed* is that the final consonant is doubled if the word has a single short vowel as in *hop* and *rob*; so *hop* becomes *hopping* and *rob* becomes *robbing*.
- → The final consonant is not doubled when the one-syllable word contains two vowels; for example *droop* becomes *drooping* and *reap* becomes *reaping*.
- → The final consonant is not doubled when the one-syllable word has a long vowel sound; for example *hurt* becomes *hurting* and *flirt* becomes *flirting*.

1 Add *-ing* to words below, using the correct spelling.

a step ______
b sleep ______
c beat ______
d heat ______
e brim ______
f break ______
g rob ______
h read ______
i rub ______
j turn ______
k drop ______
l droop ______
m hurt ______

- → With words of more than one syllable, you don't double the final consonant if the accent is on the first syllable as in *pílot, fídget, trúmpet.*
- → If the accent is on the final syllable, as in *acquít* or *regrét*, the rule is the same as for one-syllable words: the final consonant is doubled if the word has a single short vowel such as *-mit* and *-ret.*
- → The final consonant is not doubled when the one-syllable word contains two vowels, such as *-peat* and *-cruit.*

2 Add *-ed* to the words below, using the correct spelling.

a permit ______
b await ______
c repeal ______
d commit ______
e pilot ______
f acquit ______
g regret ______
h recruit ______
i admit ______
j repeat ______
k fidget ______
l prefer ______

When a noun ends in *-y*, if the letter before the *y* is a consonant, the *y* changes to *i* and you add *-es*. When the letter before the *y* is a vowel, you simply add *-s*.

3 Write the plural of the following nouns.

a ally ______

b alley ______

c valley ______

d city ______

e decoy ______

f bay ______

g turkey ______

h balcony ______

i butterfly ______

j day ______

k mercy ______

l opportunity ______

m journey ______

4 Add *-ed* to these verbs ending in *-y*, using the same rule that applies to nouns ending in *-y*.

a relay ______

b magnify ______

c fry ______

d carry ______

e bury ______

f disobey ______

g simplify ______

h dismay ______

i stay ______

j certify ______

k hurry ______

5 Most nouns ending in *-f* simply add *-s* to form the plural, for example *cliffs, cuffs, ruffs, briefs, beliefs*. But a few form their plurals differently. Write the plural form of each of the nouns below.

a half ______

b thief ______

c shelf ______

d leaf ______

e calf ______

f elf ______

g loaf ______

h self ______

i wolf ______

j wharf ______

When you add *-ing* to a verb ending in *-e*, you drop the *-e*.

6 Add *-ing* to the following verbs, using the correct spelling.

a practise ______

b write ______

c cackle ______

d hike ______

e jiggle ______

f obscure ______

g quote ______

h sense ______

i imagine ______

j care ______

k acquire ______

l commit ______

m hit ______

7 Add the suffix *-ly* to the following adjectives to make adverbs.

a reliable ______

b coy ______

c angry ______

d neglectful ______

e lengthy ______

f admirable ______

g pure ______

h weary ______

i pale ______

j liberal ______

k temporary ______

l audible ______

When you add a suffix such as *–ness*, *–ful*, *–less* or *–ly* to a word ending in *–y*, the y changes to *i*.

8 Combine the suggested suffix to each of the root words below to form a new word. Write the new word in the third column.

	Root word	Suffix	New word
a	mercy	less	
b	happy	ly	
c	plenty	ful	
d	busy	ness	
e	beauty	ful	
f	weary	ness	
g	pity	ful	
h	pity	less	
i	lazy	ness	
j	happy	ness	
k	mercy	ful	
l	drowsy	ly	
m	frosty	ly	

Memorise this rule: *i* comes before *e* – except after *c* – as long as the word rhymes with *ee*.

None of the words in the list below has *ie* because none of them rhymes with *ee*:

- foreign
- eight
- height
- leisure
- neighbour
- vein

9 Fill in the gaps in the following words with *ie* or *ei*.

a rec__ __pt
b w__ __ght
c r__ __n
d rel__ __f
e shr__ __k
f pr__ __st
g c__ __ling
h gr__ __ve
i n__ __ce
j dec__ __ve

10 It is important to be able to spell words that belong to the metalanguage of English – that is, the words you need when talking and writing about English as a subject. Below are some important ones. Some (but not all) are spelt incorrectly.

Identify the words that are spelt incorrectly and rewrite them correctly.

a rhyme ________
b paragraph ________
c gramatical ________
d writer ________
e autobiographie ________
f sonnett ________
g thesaurus ________
h punctuation ________
i rythm ________
j author ________

Name: | Due date: | Guardian signature:

15 PREFIXES

Vocabulary

A **prefix** is a word part placed before other words to form a new word (*pre* means 'before'). Thousands of words in English are formed this way. Most prefixes come from Greek and Latin, but some come from Old English and have been part of the language for centuries.

post– from Latin (means *after*): *postdate, postpone, postgraduate, postcolonial*

hyper– from Greek (means *excessive*): *hyperactive, hyperbole, hypersensitive, hyperinflation*

out– from Old English: *outnumbered, outperform, outburst, outcome*

1 Some common prefixes are listed below along with their meanings. Find two words that use each prefix. The first one has been done for you as an example.

	Prefix	Meaning	Word 1	Word 2
a	ambi–	both, two	ambivalence	ambidextrous
b	bi–	two, twice		
c	com–	with		
d	ex–	out of, formerly		
e	mis–	wrong		
f	auto–	self		
g	tele–	far, distant		
h	under–	under		

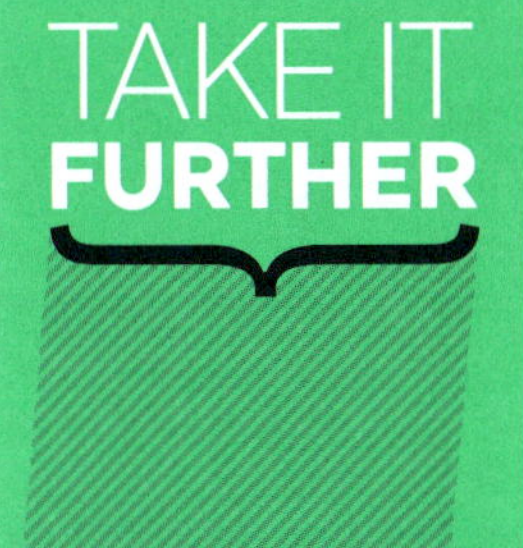

Negative prefixes change the meaning of a word to its opposite. For example, the Latin *dis–* meaning 'not' changes *like* to *dislike* (not like). Other negative prefixes include *anti–*, *de–*, *il–*, *im–*, *in–*, *ir–*, *mis–*, *non–* and *un–*.

e.g.

antibiotic	illiterate	misinform
anti-war	immortal	misunderstand
derail	impatient	non-event
deregister	indirect	nonfiction
disagree	inedible	unable
dishonest	irregular	unintelligible
illegitimate	irrelevant	

Knowing the meaning of a prefix can be a good clue to understanding an unfamiliar word.

1 Create antonyms (opposites) from the words below by adding either the prefix *dis-* (Latin, meaning 'not') or *mis-* (Latin, meaning 'wrong').

a _____charge
b _____approve
c _____able
d _____take
e _____construe
f _____robe
g _____manage
h _____took
i _____unite
j _____demeanour
k _____tasteful
l _____guide

2 Draw lines to match the negative prefixes in the first column with their meaning in the second column.

a	misuse	uneven
b	unselfish	unhappy
c	discontented	take in the wrong sense
d	immature	unable to be heard
e	inaudible	apply to the wrong purpose
f	irregular	unhealthy
g	unwell	unripe
h	illiterate	place wrongly
i	mislay	concerned for others
j	misunderstand	unable to read or write

3 Choose from the negative prefixes *il-*, *im-*, *in-* and *ir-* to form the antonyms of the following adjectives.

	Adjective	Antonym
a	sane	
b	mature	
c	regular	
d	legal	
e	possible	
f	responsible	
g	logical	

	Adjective	Antonym
h	polite	
i	reverent	
j	legible	
k	active	
l	religious	
m	moral	
n	perfect	

Name: | Due date: | Guardian signature:

16 SUFFIXES

Vocabulary

A **suffix** is a word part placed at the end of a word to change the meaning and part of speech. Suffixes (and prefixes) help us to identify parts of speech.

e.g. *critic* (noun) + *–al* (suffix) becomes *critical* (adjective)

Common suffixes used to create nouns		Common suffixes used to create verbs		Common suffixes used to create adjectives		Common suffixes used to create adverbs	
Suffix	**Example**	**Suffix**	**Example**	**Suffix**	**Example**	**Suffix**	**Example**
–acy	diplomacy	–ify	modify	–able	acceptable	–ly	mostly
–age	storage	–ise	mobilise	–al	special	–wards	afterwards
–ance	reliance			–ate	affectionate	–wise	likewise
–ation	anticipation			–ful	mindful		
–eer	engineer			–ic	fantastic		
–ist	physicist			–ious	precious		
–ness	madness			–ish	stylish		
–ory	directory			–like	childlike		
–ty	certainty			–most	foremost		
–ship	kinship			–ous	generous		

1 Add two more examples of words that use each suffix. Check your answers with a partner.

	Suffixes	Words using suffixes	Other examples
a	–acy	diplomacy	
b	–age	manage	
c	–ist	biologist	
d	–ory	victory	
e	–ship	friendship	
f	–ify	beautify	
g	–able	tolerable	
h	–ful	meaningful	
i	–ous	famous	
j	–ly	lonely	

Knowing the meaning of a suffix can be a good clue to understanding an unfamiliar word.

2 Not surprisingly, numerous words that English borrowed during the age of exploration and colonisation were unusual names of fauna and flora. Below are the names of some animals.

Draw lines to match the name of the animal in the first column with its origin in the second column. You might like to begin by making a guess and drawing your lines in pencil; you can then check your guesses using a dictionary.

	Animal name	Language of origin
a	springbok	an Australian Aboriginal language
b	llama	Malay
c	koala	an Indian language called Marathi
d	raccoon	Hindi
e	cheetah	Spanish
f	orangutan	Afrikaans
g	mongoose	Spanish
h	chamois	a South African family of languages called Khoisan
i	alligator	Arabic
j	gnu	French
k	zebra	a native American language
l	tapir	Italian
m	giraffe	Quechua, formerly the language of the Incas

Many words for foods are borrowed from other languages. The 10 foods listed below are borrowed from foreign languages. Draw lines to match the food to its language of origin.

sushi	German
cantaloupe	Dutch
tofu	Italian
pizza	Chinese
souvlaki	Spanish
bratwurst	French
profiterole	Greek
potato	Japanese
salami	Italian
scone	Italian

Name: | Due date: | Guardian signature:

19 TECHNOLOGY AND LANGUAGE CHANGE

Vocabulary

Technological and social advances have always changed language. One of the greatest changes to the English language was caused by the development of printing, which led to the standardisation of spelling. While that might seem to be a good thing, in some ways it has made the spelling of English more difficult, as the spelling has changed little over 400 years while the pronunciation of English has changed greatly, including the growth of different English accents around the world. The differences between the way a word sounds and the way it is spelt have increased.

English speakers have constantly invented or borrowed new words to cope with change. The Normans, who invaded England at the time of the Norman Conquest (in 1066), brought to the language words such as *mutton*, *veal*, *pork* and *beef*, which were used by French chefs in the kitchens of the nobility. These words were used with the words of the English farmers – *sheep*, *calf*, *pig* and *ox*. During the Renaissance, English speakers turned to Latin and Greek for new words from an expanding knowledge of science and medicine. As the British Empire expanded, new words were borrowed from almost every nation on Earth.

One of the most rapid periods of language change is the present, because of the speed of technological change. Recent developments in popular information technologies, such as email and smartphones, and the use of apps and social networking websites, have created a new language, sometimes referred to as e-language. E-language has been created out of the need for brevity in electronic messages, leading to the use of:

→ acronyms (words made up of initial letters, such as *laser* or *CAD/CAM*)
→ emoticons and smileys such as :-D or :-)) = really happy
→ the removal of vowels from txt spk.

1 Write the acronyms for the following common expressions, remembering to use numerals for some words (such as *8* for the *ate* sound).

	Expression	Acronym
a	Thank you very much	
b	In my opinion	
c	By the way	
d	For what it's worth	
e	See you later	
f	In other words	
g	Laugh out loud	
h	Frequently asked questions	
i	For your information	
j	Keep it simple, stupid	

Advances in technology lead to changes in language.

2 List the acronyms from the previous question, ranking them in order from 1 to 10 of most commonly used.

1		6	
2		7	
3		8	
4		9	
5		10	

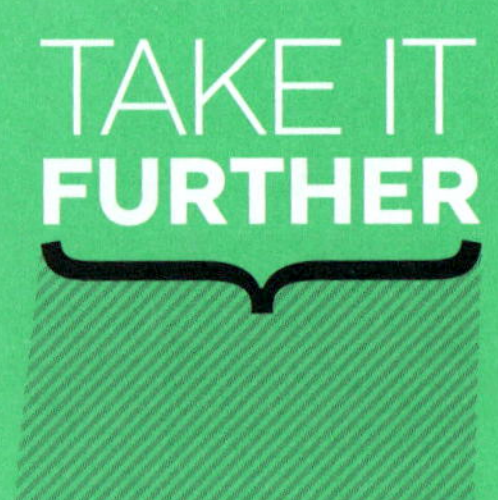

TAKE IT FURTHER

New words are formed in all kinds of ways. Some involve taking existing words and using them as new parts of speech. For example, 'Google' has become a verb: 'I'll google that topic and see what I can find out.' Others involve:

- → using existing words in new combinations
- → using old words with new meanings
- → blending two existing words to make a new word
- → adding an affix to a word to create a new meaning
- → making a new word from Latin or Greek roots
- → making a new word out of an acronym.

Write these fairly recent new words under the appropriate heading in the table.

astronaut	emoticon	metrosexual	spam
carbon footprint	fashionista	newbie	spin doctor
carjack	gay	nimby	tweet
cosmonaut	gym bunny	shopaholic	LOL
cyberbully	googleganger	shovel-ready	voicemail
SWOT	junk mail	social networking	

Ways of creating new words	Examples
Using existing words in new combinations	
Using old words with new meanings	
Adding an affix to a word	
Making a new word out of an acronym	
Blending two existing words	
Making a new word from Latin or Greek roots	

Name: | Due date: | Guardian signature:

20 SYNONYMS AND ANTONYMS

Vocabulary

A **synonym** is a word that has a similar meaning to another word. Synonyms communicate shades of meaning. They are the same part of speech as the word they replace.

The film was *exciting*. (adjective)
Synonyms: *thrilling, stimulating, enthralling* (adjectives)
I expressed my *joy* over her achievement. (noun)
Synonyms: *delight, pleasure, happiness* (nouns)
The pioneers *occupied* the fertile valleys. (verb)
Synonyms: *settled, conquered* (verbs)

An **antonym** is a word that has the opposite meaning to another word. Antonyms are also the same part of speech as the word they replace.

The *tall* dancer won a prize. (adjective)
Antonyms: *short, small, little, petite* (adjectives)

Many antonyms are formed by adding prefixes such as *un–* (*unsatisfactory*), *im–* (*immodest*) and *dis–* (*dissatisfied*).

1 Look at the words in capital letters on each line below. From the four words following it, circle its synonym – the one that has almost the same meaning.

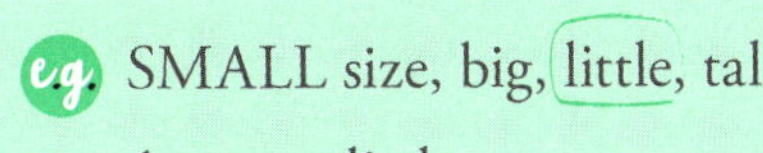

a WEIGHTY light, heavy, kilogram, measurement
b TIRED bored, weary, exhaustion, tiring
c WEALTHY rich, generous, well-meaning, healthy
d CHEAP dear, inexpensive, cheerful, miserable
e ROUGH tough, gentle, tactile, coarse
f WEAK strong, tired, little, feeble
g POWERFUL mighty, proud, severe, political
h SLEEK satin, smooth, pretty, rough
i STURDY puny, muscular, strong, fitness
j ANCIENT ancestor, old, age, youthful
k GIGANTIC enormous, tiny, size, sturdy
l INVISIBLE obscure, secret, hidden, noticeable

Appropriate synonyms and antonyms express fine distinctions in meaning.

2 Draw a line to match the word in the first column with its antonym in the second column.

a	certain	pessimistic
b	clean	danger
c	optimistic	lighten
d	happy	doubtful
e	joy	trusting
f	laughter	private
g	safety	dirty
h	public	complexity
i	darken	sad
j	simplicity	sorrow
k	jealous	tears

3 Synonyms and antonyms are always the same part of speech. Underline the antonym in each of the following sets and write it in a sentence to show clearly its meaning.

a joy, boredom, sorrow, fun, pleasure

b laughter, merriment, complaint, laziness, tension

c safety, danger, disaster, security, loss

a ______________________________

b ______________________________

c ______________________________

____

TAKE IT FURTHER

Synonyms indicate fine differences in meaning. Rearrange the following groups of adjectives in order of intensity, going from the weakest to the strongest meaning.

a uneasy, terrified, frightened ______________________________

b funny, amusing, hilarious ______________________________

c distraught, agitated, upset ______________________________

d tall, gigantic, towering ______________________________

e joyful, ecstatic, happy ______________________________

f lovable, likable, adorable ______________________________

g naughty, bad, evil ______________________________

h hot, sweltering, warm ______________________________

i ugly, unattractive, grotesque ______________________________

j delicious, tasty, scrumptious ______________________________

Name: | Due date: | Guardian signature:

21 EMOTIVE LANGUAGE

Vocabulary

Nearly all words carry emotive connotations; that is, words can have a meaning in addition to their explicit or primary meaning. A possible connotation of 'HOME' is a place of warmth, comfort and affection. Think too of a word such as *mother*. It could be used literally in a legal document to describe a female parent in a family relationship, but in most contexts it is loaded with emotion. A newspaper might report that: 'A young mother was killed in a car accident', not 'A 24-year-old woman was killed in a car accident', to convey the emotional force of the word.

Connotations can be positive or negative. The word *home* has positive connotations, while *hovel* has negative connotations of a small squalid dwelling.

Our speech and writing would be dull if words did not carry emotional connotations and our choice of emotive language allows us to convey attitudes and opinions.

1 In the pairs of sentences below, you will find the same word repeated. In one sentence the word is used in an emotive way. Underline the emotive sentence in each pair.

a i The bottle must be *shaken* before opening.

ii She was badly *shaken* by the accident.

b i She has a *sweet*, innocent manner.

ii He eats a lot of *sweet* food.

c i The basket is *empty*.

ii He is an *empty*-headed boy.

d i A precious *antique* was offered at the auction.

ii She's so old, she's *antique*!

e i They have many *common* interests.

ii Her speech is very *common*.

f i The silverware is *dull* with age.

ii He has a *dull* mind.

2 The connotations of words can be positive or negative. For the sentences on the following page, choose the positive synonym for the first-person sentence (the 'I') and the negative synonym for the third-person sentence (the 'he' or 'she') from the pair of synonyms given.

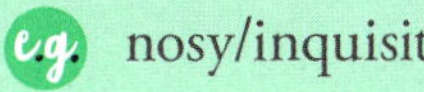

e.g. nosy/inquisitive

i I am inquisitive.

ii He is nosy.

When choosing words in your writing, it is important to be aware of their emotive connotations.

a modest/timid

i I have a __________________ manner.

ii She has a __________________ manner.

b furtive/silent

i I was __________________ about my intentions.

ii He was __________________ about his intentions.

c childlike/childish

i My manners have been described as pleasingly __________________.

ii His manners have been described as __________________.

d firm/stubborn

i I am quite __________________ when I make up my mind.

ii She is quite __________________ when she makes up her mind.

e famous/notorious

i I am __________________ since that story was published in the newspapers.

ii He is __________________ since that story was published in the newspapers.

f up-to-date/newfangled

i I like to always have __________________ technology.

ii She likes to always have __________________ technology.

g thrifty/miserly

i I have always been __________________ with money.

ii He has always been __________________ with money.

h commanding/dictatorial

i My leadership is characterised by my __________________ manner.

ii Her leadership is characterised by her __________________ manner.

TAKE IT FURTHER

Advertisers use emotive language. For example, a new car is a '*dream* machine'. In the examples below, underline the advertiser's language.

a Do you long to regain your (former/old) (slender/skinny/thin) beauty? Jody's Gym has a fitness (plan/regime) just for you.

b Hurry out to Parramatta Road for the best deal in (second-hand/preloved) cars.

c There's nothing lovelier than (velvet/unblemished) skin that has been (warmed/toasted) by the summer sun to a (deep tan/golden bloom).

Name: | Due date: | Guardian signature:

22 RESEARCHING LANGUAGE

Vocabulary

USING A DICTIONARY

A **dictionary** is a book or online resource that provides the meanings of words in alphabetical order. Most dictionaries also show how to spell a word (with any alternative spelling) and the part of speech of the word (noun, verb, adjective, adverb, pronoun, conjunction).

Bigger dictionaries explain how to pronounce the word and include its origin and history.

1 Use a dictionary to find out the precise meanings of the following words. Then learn their meanings and use the words in a sentence in the space provided. Check each other's answers.

a pugnacious

b parsimonious

c radical

d conservative

e reconciliation

2 Use a dictionary to look up then explain the pronunciation of the following words.

e.g. gauge — Rhymes with 'rage'.

honourable — The stress is on the first syllable, 'ho'. The 'h' is silent.

a formidable

b personnel

Dictionaries, thesauruses and usage guides are essential tools for good writers.

c wrath

d centenary

3 Study and sport require regular *practice/practise*. I also *practice/practise* my music each day.

a Circle what you think are the correct words in italics above.
b Use a dictionary to find out the difference between *practice* and *practise*.
c Check your answer again.

USING A THESAURUS

A **thesaurus** is a rich collection of words and their related ideas. You can find both synonyms and antonyms for words or phrases in a thesaurus. It is a valuable reference for anyone who wants to write and speak effective and precise English. The most useful and best-known is *Roget's Thesaurus*. However, there are others, including online thesauruses.

Some thesauruses are in simple alphabetical order. *Roget's* is more difficult to use but will give you a much richer range of words. To use *Roget's Thesaurus* follow these steps:

→ There is an alphabetical list of words at the back of the thesaurus. Look up the word to select synonyms or antonyms closest in meaning. Next to the meaning will be a number.
→ Look up the number that relates to that meaning. (Note that the number does *not* refer to a page number, but to the number for that entry in the front section of the book.)
→ Choose carefully the word or expression that is most appropriate to your requirements.

Beside each word in the table below, write three associated words from your thesaurus. The first one has been done for you. Note that there are many possible answers.

	Alphabetical order	Associated word (1)	Associated word (2)	Associated word (3)
a	alienate	reject	isolate	marginalise
b	apprehend			
c	germinate			
d	mediate			
e	mentor			
f	propose			
g	renown			
h	requisition			
i	retrieve			
j	sympathy			

Name: | Due date: | Guardian signature:

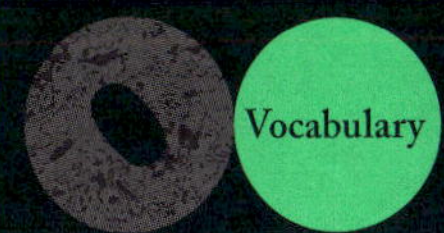

REVISION TEST 5

1 Add a prefix to change the meaning of the following words.

a The boy was __________active in class.

b I am only interested in the __________natural world.

c She is a most __________adventurous girl.

d The girls looked __________similar.

e My favourite genre is __________fiction.

f The U-turn that Jerry just made was __________legal.

g The teenagers were acting very __________maturely for their age.

2 Write three words using the prefixes given.

a *tele* = distant ______________________________

b *pre* = before ______________________________

c *semi* = half, part ______________________________

d *trans* = across, change ______________________________

e *micro* = small, minute ______________________________

f *bi* = two ______________________________

3 Write a synonym for each of the following words.

a	transfer	__________	f	proceed	__________
b	anticipate	__________	g	recount	__________
c	connect	__________	h	hilarious	__________
d	import	__________	i	functional	__________
e	acceptable	__________	j	plain	__________

4 Write an antonym for each of the following words.

a	serenity	__________	e	peaceful	__________
b	distance	__________	f	sociable	__________
c	solitude	__________	g	beautiful	__________
d	loneliness	__________	h	famous	__________

5 Underline the eight suffixes in the following real estate advertisement for a luxury home.

In this wonderful mansion, built for your every need, you will enjoy the lifestyle of the rich and famous. Gorgeous windows facing north greet the sun all day. The enormous garden will give you peace and happiness in an urban environment.

6 In each pair of synonyms below there is one neutral and one emotive word. Underline the emotive word in each pair.

a fat – plump

b elderly – decrepit

c young – juvenile

d bossy – assertive

e inquisitive – curious

f extravagant – generous

g bold – reckless

h skinny – slim

i aggressive – determined

j quiet – taciturn

7 Write *true* or *false* after each of the following statements about language.

a The majority of the words used in everyday speech come from Old English. ___________

b Acronyms were invented to make text messaging easier. ___________

c Most names for scientific studies come from Latin or Greek. ___________

d The standardisation of English spelling meant all English speakers could share written texts. ___________

e The standardisation of English spelling meant that, over time, the gap widened between the way many words were pronounced. ___________

f Young people who use text speak constantly are losing the ability to write properly. ___________

g Living languages are steadily changing. ___________

h Early colonists to Australia adopted words from Aboriginal languages for unfamiliar flora and fauna. ___________

i Australia did not have its own Aussie accent until the mid-twentieth century. ___________

Name: Due date: Guardian signature:

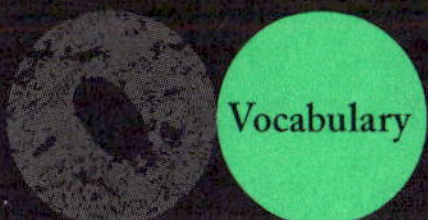

SPELLING FOCUS 2

1 Circle the words below that have a double letter when the last letter of the prefix is the same as the first letter of the main word.

a unnoticed / unimaginable

b dissatisfied / disobey

c underrate / undertake

d overreach / overlook

e immortal / improbable

2 Which of the following negative prefixes needs a double letter? Add a second letter if it is required.

a dis__organise

b il__egitimate

c im__ovable

d dis__honest

e dis__ervice

f in__excusable

g im__probable

h un__atural

i un__occupied

j mis__use

3 All the words below have a silent letter. The same letter is missing from all seven words. What is the missing letter?

cor__s

__salm

__sychopath

__seudonym

__terodactyl

ras__berry

4 Here are some more words with a silent letter. Write the correct letter; for example, *k* goes in *__nit*.

a __now

b lis__ener

c mor__gage

d mus__le

e play__right

f plum__er

g __neumonia

h __seudonym

i __naw

j __sychologist

	Singular	Plural
h	sheep	
i	echo	
j	foot	
k	half	
l	hobby	
m	loaf	
n	man	
o	mouse	
p	parenthesis	
q	phenomenon	
r	woman	

12 A tricky part of spelling is whether or not to double a letter in a word. For example, a common mistake is not doubling the *c* in *occasion*. Rewrite the following words correctly in the second column. (Note that some spaces have been left where a double letter is *not* required.) Use a dictionary if you are unsure of the spelling or meaning.

a ac__om__odation ____________

b ad__res__ ____________

c dif__er__ence ____________

d excel__ent ____________

e ful__fil__ ____________

f inflam__able ____________

g oc__ur__ ____________

h par__al__el__ ____________

i prof__es__or ____________

j question__aire ____________

13 Here are the main words for the metalanguage of English – that is, the words you need when talking and writing about English as a subject. In each case, one letter has been left out. Write the missing letters in the spaces provided.

ass__nance	begin__ing	diction__ry	gramm__r
all__teration	meta__hor	nov__list	play__right
r__ythm	auxil__ary	adjectiv__l	simil__

Name:	Due date:	Guardian signature:

23 PUNCTUATING SENTENCE ENDINGS

Punctuation

Full stops (.) are used to indicate the end of a sentence that is a statement.

e.g. Roald Dahl wrote many stories with a twist.

Question marks (?) are used to indicate the end of a sentence that asks a question.

e.g. Are you willing to take on a part-time job?

Exclamation marks (!) are used at the end of a sentence that is exclaimed or commanded in order to:

→ express strong emotion	e.g. 'Ouch! That really hurt me!'
→ indicate calling or shouting	e.g. 'Robert!', 'Carn the Pies!'
→ suggest emphasis or a strong tone of voice.	e.g. 'Do not touch that switch or else there will be trouble!'

1 Playscripts often use a variety of sentence types and end-of-sentence punctuation marks to convey drama and atmosphere. Add full stops, question marks and exclamation marks where required in the following extract from the playscript *'Truth or Dare?'* Jane is angry with her parents and brother for moving house.

IAN: Where's Jane__

SANDRA (*calling*): Jane__

PETER: She's still outside__

SANDRA: Still__ Come in, love__

IAN (*calling*): Jane, come in and give us a hand__

Jane ignores him and sits on the veranda steps.

SANDRA (*worried, to Ian*): She just refuses to come in__ She says she won't set foot in this house__

IAN: What__

SANDRA: She says it's not like our old home__

PETER: She reckons she's going to run away – all the way back across the country__

IAN (*annoyed*): Stop being so childish, Jane__ Grow up__

PETER (*loudly*): Yeah, act your age, Jane__

SANDRA: Why don't you just come in__

Deriu, Laura & Jordan, Noel 1996, *Truth or Dare?*, Unpublished.

All sentences end with either a full stop, a question mark or an exclamation mark.

2 The opening of a short story must capture the reader's interest immediately. Below is an extract from the opening section of *Sticks and Stones and Such-Like* by Sunil Badami, in which he reflects on being bullied and his mother's advice. Badami uses a range of punctuation marks to create different types of sentences and interest for the reader. Identify the punctuation by completing the tasks underneath the extract.

> My mother would always say, 'Stones and sticks and such-like can only shake your skeletons. Just rise over it!' Which was even more irritating than if it had been said correctly. She was right though – after being called anything and everything enough times, I stopped wincing…
>
> … But the one thing that always got under my skin was my own name. Sunil. My mother and Indian relatives pronounce it 'Soo-neel'; my own broad accent makes it 'Sir-neil'.
>
> SUN-ill, SOON-ull, SAN-eel, I've heard 'em all. 'Sunil? Like senile?' Or that old playground favourite: 'Sunil? Like banana *peel*?' If I had a dollar for every time, how many rupees would that make?
>
> Badami, Sunil 2008, 'Sticks and Stones and Such-Like', in Alice Pung (ed), *Growing up Asian in Australia*, Black Inc, p. 9.

a Draw circles around the full stops.

b Draw squares around the question marks.

c Draw triangles around the exclamation marks.

d How would you describe the atmosphere conveyed by the combination of punctuation marks in this extract? How does this author convey humour through using punctuation marks? Are there any other language strategies used by the author? What is their effect? Discuss these with a partner.

e Look at the sentences and punctuation used in the advice given by Sunil's mum. What is the author trying to suggest about her personality? Discuss with a partner.

f What fiction text are you reading now? Read the opening paragraph and note the type of punctuation used. Describe to a partner the atmosphere created by the particular combination of punctuation marks used.

Develop a short dramatic script between two characters using a range of sentences requiring full stops, question marks and exclamation marks. Choose any of the pairs of opening lines provided.

Decide on the who (characters), where (setting) and what (plot) of your dramatic script. Also, decide on the genre of your script: will it be a comedy, tragedy, mystery, sci fi or another genre? Include instructions in brackets about how the lines are to be delivered and any accompanying actions.

Rehearse and perform your script for the class.

A: I have something important to tell you.
B: What is it?

or

A: Did you see (hear) that?
B: No! What happened?

or

A: Have we got any other options?
B: It looks like there are some possibilities.

Name: | Due date: | Guardian signature:

24 COMMAS

Punctuation

Commas (,) are used to:

→ separate items in a list

e.g. The special offer includes a hotdog, large fries, a cake and a soft drink.

→ separate an introductory word, noun phrase or clause at the beginning of a sentence

e.g. Although it was raining, we went camping.

→ separate an explanatory phrase, clause or non-essential information within a sentence

e.g. My grandmother, who is now in her eighties, was the Women's Racing Car Champion in 1950.

→ separate a series of clauses.

e.g. We packed the car, picked up our friends, stopped at the shops for provisions and then set off for our camping trip.

(Note: Commas are also used in the punctuation of direct speech – see Unit 29.)

Circle the commas in the sentences below and suggest why commas have been used in each case by stating one of the rules listed above.

e.g. Melinda, who is known for her sense of humour, was the class clown.

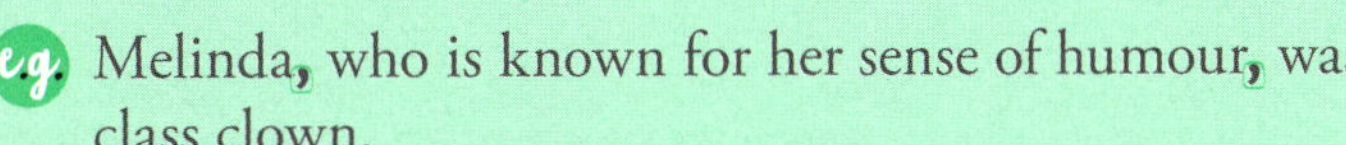

Explanation: To separate an explanation within the sentence

a Despite several warnings from the police, the crowd continued to jeer at the politicians.

b The activities included swimming, snorkelling, windsurfing and fishing.

c Halt, who goes there?

d The house, which was in a derelict state, was bulldozed.

e The street, which did not show up on the GPS navigator, was impossible to find!

f Generally, you should do warm-up exercises before playing any sport.

Commas can never be used in place of full stops.

g Notable Australian authors include Isobel Carmody, Jackie French, Morris Gleitzman and Wendy Orr.

h Ocean Grove, which is situated on the Bellarine Peninsula in Victoria, has a safe surf beach.

i Students are prohibited from bringing mobile phones, calculators and other electronic devices into the exam room.

j The athletes were warming up, the spectators were taking their seats and excitement was building.

k In view of the conditions, the bushwalk was cancelled.

l As a rule, people don't go beyond the small fence, the citrus trees or the vegetable patch.

Henry Lawson (1867–1922) is a significant author in Australia's literary heritage. Lawson's writing is vivid and his lengthy sentences contain a variety of types of phrases and clauses to build a detailed picture of life in the bush.

Read the opening extract below from his short story 'The Drover's Wife' about a family's encounter with a snake. Unfortunately, the commas have fallen out of the text. Add commas where appropriate so that the story makes sense; you will need 16 commas.

The two-roomed house is built of round timber slabs and stringy bark and floored with split slabs. A big bark kitchen standing at one end is larger than the house itself verandah included.

Bush all round – bush with no horizon for the country is flat. No ranges in the distance. The bush consists of stunted rotten native apple trees. No undergrowth. Nothing to relieve the eye save the darker green of a few sheoaks which are sighing above the narrow almost waterless creek. Nineteen miles to the nearest sign of civilization – a shanty on a main road.

The drover an ex-squatter is away with sheep. His wife and children are left here alone.

Four ragged dried-up-looking children are playing about the house. Suddenly one of them yells: 'Snake! Mother here's a snake!'

The gaunt sun-browned bushwoman dashes from the kitchen snatches her baby from the ground holds it on her left hip and reaches for a stick.

'Where is it?'

Lawson, Henry 1892, 'The drover's wife'.

Name: | Due date: | Guardian signature:

25 APOSTROPHES

Punctuation

An **apostrophe for contraction (')** is used when one or more letters have been omitted from a word.

 Unfortunately, *I'll* have to reply that I *can't* attend the party.
I'll = I will; *can't* = cannot

An **apostrophe for possession** is used to show ownership. It can:

→ show possession in a singular noun by adding *'s* to the noun

e.g. the student's assignment = the assignment of the student

→ show possession in a regular plural noun by adding *s'* to the noun

e.g. the neighbours' Christmas street party = the Christmas street party of the neighbours

→ show possession in an irregular plural noun by adding *'s* to the noun

e.g. the women's cars = the cars of the women

→ show possession in a singular noun already ending in *–s* by adding either *'s* or just *'*.

Be consistent in your application of the apostrophe in this situation – choose one way and stick to it.

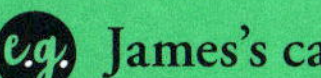 James's cat *or* James' cat

1 Write the contractions below in full words.

	Contraction	Full words
a	it's	
b	won't	
c	should've	
d	can't	
e	we'll	

	Contraction	Full words
f	aren't	
g	could've	
h	isn't	
i	they'd	
j	I'll	

2 Write the contracted form of the words below.

	Full words	Contraction
a	I had/would	
b	would not	
c	we have	
d	let us	
e	you are	

	Full words	Contraction
f	would have	
g	of the clock	
h	were not	
i	do not	
j	was not	

Apostrophes are never used to show that a noun is plural.

3 Each sentence below contains two contracted words with the apostrophe omitted. Rewrite each contraction, inserting the missing apostrophe then write out each contraction in full words.

> *e.g.* I know I couldve, but I didnt!
>
> **Answer:** could've – could have; didn't – did not

a Thats unfair - theyve gotten away with it again!

b Youll have to miss out as you didnt submit your application on time.

c Heres an offer you cant refuse!

d Theyd have joined us if theyd been given enough notice.

4 Rewrite the following sentences, adding apostrophes of possession where necessary.

a Several guests personal belongings were stolen during the companys party!

b Jennifers holiday was shortened due to her parents change of plan.

c The congregations behaviour was respectful at the politicians funeral.

d The pianists extraordinary performance held the audiences interest for over two hours.

Create a do-it-yourself apostrophes reference sheet by making a poster based on the following table. Begin by writing in all the contracted words you can think of. Check your spelling and punctuation for accuracy. Display your poster in the classroom and refer to it when you are unsure about using apostrophes.

Full words	Contraction
I will	I'll

Name: | Due date: | Guardian signature:

26 COLONS AND SEMICOLONS

Punctuation

A **colon (:)** is used to introduce a list – especially when the list is preceded by *the following* or *as follows*.

e.g. You may wish to bring the following optional items on the hike: a camera, binoculars, insect repellent and sunglasses.

Add these groceries to the shopping list: milk, bread, orange juice and peanut butter.

A colon is also used when you are giving specific examples or details.

e.g. They mostly publish educational books: textbooks for secondary schools and readers for primary schools.

A colon is also used to introduce a quotation.

e.g. Abraham Lincoln's famous speech begins: 'Fourscore and seven years ago …'

A **semicolon (;)** is used to indicate a pause longer than a comma but shorter than a full stop. It can be used to separate related main ideas that are not connected by a conjunction.

e.g. The Terminator was an invincible warrior; he was like a one-soldier army.

My sister left home last year; I miss her.

In both of these examples a full stop could have been used instead of the semicolon to separate the two ideas, or a conjunction and a comma could have been used:

e.g. My sister left home last year. I miss her.

My sister left home last year, and I miss her.

Using the semicolon makes it clear that the ideas are closely connected, and it also draws attention to the second idea.

Semicolons are also used to mark off items in a list, when commas alone would be confusing.

e.g. Add these groceries to the shopping list: bread, preferably wholemeal; milk, low-fat, of course; orange juice, fresh and unsweetened; and crunchy peanut butter.

Do not use a capital letter after a colon or a semicolon, except when the colon is used to introduce a quotation that begins with a capital letter.

1 Using a coloured pen or pencil, insert a colon where necessary in the sentences below.

- **a** You will need the following ingredients eggs, flour and sugar.
- **b** A former Australian prime minister was much criticised for saying 'Life wasn't meant to be easy.'
- **c** On Sunday night, Jordan placed the following in his schoolbag textbooks, pencil case, folder, history project model and his tablet.
- **d** The room was sparsely furnished a chair, a desk and a bookcase.
- **e** Students were given these instructions line up, sing the national anthem and file into the assembly hall.

A colon is frequently used to introduce a list.

f When I went to the library I borrowed several books *To Kill a Mockingbird, Holes* and *Blueback*.

g My home group class includes students from a variety of cultural backgrounds Indian, Greek, Vietnamese, Italian, Chinese, Dutch and South African.

2 Correct each run-on sentence below by inserting a semicolon where necessary to emphasise the connection between ideas.

a It's an exciting lesson plan I think it will work and the students will enjoy the fun role-plays at the end.

b The coach chose a new player for the final he had just kicked 10 goals in the reserves and had been voted best player on the ground.

c Biodegradable liquid soap is available at the camp site it is suitable as shampoo as well.

d It was a day of extreme temperatures everyone was feeling sluggish.

e I didn't mean to break the glass it just slipped right out of my hand!

f Several guests had property stolen during the party many lost mobile phones.

g Jenny's holidays were unexpectedly shortened her mother was unwell.

h It was a glorious summer's day there were no clouds to be seen.

3 Insert one missing colon and one missing semicolon in the following passage.

> Dickens is famous for his balanced sentences. One of my favourites is this quotation from *A Tale of Two Cities* 'There were a king with a large jaw and a queen with a plain face, on the throne of England there were a king with a large jaw and a queen with a fair face, on the throne of France.

You have been commissioned by Awesome Safari Tours to edit the text for the webpage advertising its Red Centre tour. The company has supplied you with the text. Review the text below and add semicolons and colons where they are needed. You will need to add three colons and seven semicolons. To help you, boxes have been added where the punctuation is required.

AWESOME RED CENTRE SAFARI TOURS

Join us for the ultimate Australian Red Centre adventure expedition ☐ an unforgettable tour experience visiting the icons of Central Australia.

Your tour will stop over at Uluru for a sunset and sunrise ☐ hike the Valley of Winds in the Olgas ☐ visit Kings Canyon, Glen Helen and Ormiston Gorge ☐ explore the MacDonnell Ranges ☐ check out the Finke River ☐ and travel to Palm Valley and Standley Chasm.

This is an adventure tour with all the comforts ☐ private bush camp sites, campfire cooking and sleeping under the southern stars in a true-blue Aussie swag. All meals on tour are provided from lunch on day one to lunch on day five ☐ let us know if you have special dietary requirements.

You will need to bring the following essential gear ☐ walking shoes or boots, sun hat, polar fleece jacket, light jumper, light trousers, thermal underwear, socks and some T-shirts. If it rains, we add a rain jacket ☐ if it is warm we strip off layers.

Name: | Due date: | Guardian signature:

27 DASHES AND BRACKETS

Punctuation

Dashes and brackets are used to organise additional information conveyed within a sentence. Dashes may be used singly or in pairs, depending on their function in the sentence. Brackets, also known as parentheses, are always used in pairs.

Dashes (-) can be used like colons to signify a summary, a series or list, or an explanation. Colons are preferred in formal writing but dashes are frequently used in this way in less formal communications.

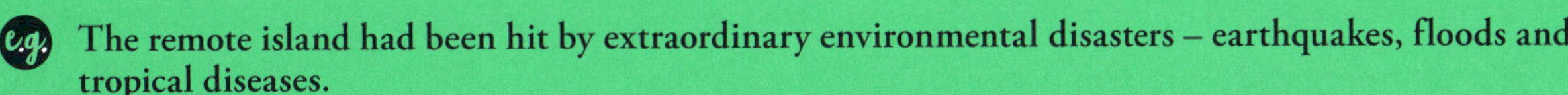

e.g. The remote island had been hit by extraordinary environmental disasters – earthquakes, floods and tropical diseases.

Don't forget to bring wet weather gear – boots, a raincoat and a waterproof cover for your backpack.

If the list is enclosed within the sentence, it might need two dashes.

e.g. Don't forget to bring wet weather gear – boots, a raincoat and a waterproof cover for your backpack – and make sure that you are on time for the bus.

Dashes indicate breaks in speech or thought. They are used in this way mainly in dialogue.

e.g. 'I – I – I think I can see a – a – a – Help!' shouted Shaggy at Scooby.

I told the truth – you've got to believe me – I always tell the absolute truth.

Brackets enclose additional information such as explanations, examples and reference information within a sentence.

e.g. The committee (made up of representatives from all states and territories) voted to develop the new program.

The euro is the official currency of France (current exchange rate 1EUR = 1.44AUD).

Note that commas or dashes can also be used in a similar way to mark off additional information in a sentence. It is often a matter of personal choice.

e.g. The committee, made up of representatives from all states and territories, voted to develop the new program.

Brackets indicate numbers or letters in a list.

e.g. After missing the train to the CBD, we didn't know whether we should (a) wait half an hour for the next one, (b) begin walking or (c) return home.

Brackets can be used to provide a reference within a sentence.

e.g. You can find more information on this topic in your textbook (see Chapters 8 and 9).

In a play script, brackets signify stage directions about setting, voice and action. The stage direction is usually printed in italics.

e.g. Sam (menacingly): I'm telling on you.

Alissa: Don't you dare! (*Makes a threatening gesture*)

Both dashes and brackets can be used to indicate an aside or an afterthought.

e.g. Most schools – but not my school – allow students to go home if the temperature hits 40 degrees.

Most schools (but not my school) allow students to go home if the temperature hits 40 degrees.

Choice of punctuation can depend on the nature of your text, especially on the degree of formality.

1 Add brackets where appropriate in the following sentences.

- **a** Download the PDF manual from our website for quick set-up instructions for your new phone see page 3.
- **b** Jack and Raleena had been researching the Bayeux Tapestry a 70-metre-long tapestry depicting the Battle of Hastings in 1066.
- **c** Making the soup takes 10 minutes and is as easy as a boiling water, b adding a chicken-flavoured stock cube, and c adding a chopped carrot and a handful of short noodles.
- **d** The OECD Organisation for Economic Co-operation and Development reports regularly on comparative student performances.
- **e** Uluru one of Australia's most sacred sites used to be known as Ayers Rock.
- **f** You can get there easily by bus Number 22 is the most direct route.

2 Add dashes where appropriate in the following sentences.

- **a** If you are interested in doing a hobby well writing, sports, cooking, debating and such you will need to practise.
- **b** 'I feel s s s sick just l l l looking down!' stammered Najaf as he attempted to climb up to the flying fox platform.
- **c** There is a local café I forget its name that serves gluten-free products.
- **d** I need you to pick up some groceries from the corner store milk, eggs, bacon and some fresh bread.
- **e** Police were shocked at the state of the crime scene furniture had been overturned, drawers emptied out and a threatening message had been sprayed across a wall.
- **f** Robin Hood a well-known medieval folk hero who is immortalised in many ballads was an outlaw who lived in Sherwood Forest.

1 Brackets can sometimes be replaced by other punctuation. In the following sentences, you could use commas or dashes instead of brackets. Mark with a cross where the commas or brackets would go.

- **a** The OECD Organisation for Economic Co-operation and Development reports regularly on comparative student performances.
- **b** Uluru one of Australia's most sacred sites used to be known as Ayers Rock.
- **c** Learning belly dancing an ancient art form has become popular in recent years.
- **d** Parentheses also called brackets are useful punctuation marks.

2 Underline the two sentences in which a colon could be used instead of a dash.

- **a** There is a local café – I forget its name – that serves gluten-free products.
- **b** I need you to pick up some groceries – milk, eggs, bacon and some fresh bread.
- **c** Police were shocked at the state of the crime scene – furniture had been overturned, drawers emptied out and a threatening message had been sprayed across a wall.

Name: | Due date: | Guardian signature:

28 PUNCTUATING TITLES

Punctuation

The titles of texts and other works with titles (such as paintings or sculptures) must be clearly indicated in a piece of writing. Some titles are enclosed in quotation marks, others are underlined (or italicised in printed text). The system below is commonly accepted.

→ The titles of the following types of texts are underlined in handwriting or italicised in print: nonfiction and fiction books, plays, films, musical works, newspaper and magazine titles, television series and works of art.

→ The titles of the following types of texts are enclosed in single quotation marks: short stories, chapter titles, single episodes in a television series, poems, songs, articles, essays and lectures.

1 Punctuate and/or underline the titles in the following sentences appropriately.

a The students were required to read the chapters titled Leaving home , Doubts and A last request for homework.

b The librarian recommended that students read Roald Dahl's short story Lamb to the Slaughter in his collection called Tales of the Unexpected.

c Tom used The Photo Book extensively in preparing his presentation about the history of photography.

d This year, the students will study the novel In the Lake of the Woods and the film Look Both Ways.

e Roy Lichtenstein was an influential pop artist who used the comic style effectively in works such as As I Opened Fire.

f The senior class went to see a performance of Shakespeare's Macbeth at the Central Theatre.

g The music chosen for the funeral was Pachelbel's Canon and Albinoni's Adagio.

h The senior students performed a theatrical reading of T.S. Eliot's poem The Hollow Men.

i Mum usually buys the magazine The Big Issue because she enjoys the regular articles in it such as Your Say and My Word.

j Some of the top animations of the 21st century include Toy Story 3, Monsters Inc, Finding Nemo and Ratatouille.

k We love watching Australia's Got Talent because it gives ordinary people a chance to show off their entertainment skills.

l Our local newspaper, The Melbourne Weekly, reported that the crime rate in the area was down.

m My brother only reads sports magazines such as Skater and Surfer.

n For my detention punishment I had to write a 500-word essay on 10 reasons why I shouldn't play pranks.

o After guiding the youth congregation through some tough team challenges, the pastor gave a sermon called Learning to handle life responsibly.

Underlining in handwriting is represented by italics in printing.

2 Respond to the following questions by giving an appropriate title. Remember to punctuate your title correctly.

a Best film?

b Worst film?

c Best novel?

d Worst novel?

e Best song?

f Worst song?

Work with a partner. Go to the library and find titles for the following types of texts and materials. Write down the titles and punctuate them accurately. If you have time, read, watch or listen to one of the titles you have listed.

- a documentary DVD
- a magazine
- a classical music CD
- a novel for young adults by an Australian author
- a short story from an anthology of stories (you will need to write down both the title of the story and of the anthology)
- a work of art
- a newspaper
- a poem from a collection of poems (you will need to write down both the title of the poem and of the collection)
- the DVD of a film
- an audio tape/CD reading of a novel
- a chapter title from a novel or nonfiction text (you will need to write down both the title of the chapter and of the novel or nonfiction text from which it comes)
- a song
- a newspaper or magazine article
- a playscript
- a musical score.

Name:	Due date:	Guardian signature:

29 PUNCTUATING SPEECH

Punctuation

Quotation marks (", ') in speech (sometimes called speech marks or inverted commas) are used in pairs ('…') to enclose the words, sounds and exclamations actually spoken by a person. Observe the following conventions when using quotation marks and direct speech:

→ enclose all the spoken words in the quotation marks
→ begin the first word with a capital letter
→ enclose all punctuation marks inside the quotation marks when they are part of the speaker's words (including commas, question marks and exclamation marks)
→ start a new line for each individual speaker.

e.g. 'Knock, knock,' she called.
'Who's there?' he asked.
She said, 'Avenue.'
'Avenue who?' he asked.
'Avenue heard,' she laughed, 'this joke before?'

1 Add quotation marks and appropriate punctuation where required in the following sentences.

a He said Knock knock
Who s there she asked
Justin he said
Justin who she enquired
Justin the neighbourhood he chuckled and thought I d drop in

b Knock knock she announced
Who s there he asked
Arch she said
Arch who
Bless you she giggled

c Knock knock he said
She asked Who s there
Little old lady
She asked Little old lady who
Where did you learn to yodel he said surprised

When quoting direct speech, you must use quotation marks.

2 Rewrite the following conversation with correct speech punctuation and layout.

Oh, yes Adam said. And he asked why we didn't go to the police if we suspected Mike. Something like that she agreed. But I don't think he was altogether satisfied with my answers. I wonder why Adam said with a sniff.

McRobbie, David 1992, *Mandragora*, Mammouth Australia, p. 209.

TAKE IT FURTHER

Reported speech is a summary of what a speaker said but does *not* use quotation marks or the actual words spoken by a speaker.

e.g. (Direct speech): Mia said, 'I'm going to join the debating team.'
(Reported speech): Mia said that she wanted to join the debating team.

Rewrite the sentences below as reported speech.

e.g. Enrico said, 'I want to visit Italy to see my grandmother but my soccer tour made it impossible.'

Answer: Enrico said *he wanted* to visit Italy to see *his* grandmother but *his* soccer tour made it impossible.

The italics show the changes in person (third person: *he* and *his*) and tense (past tense: *wanted*) needed to make this sentence reported speech.

a Maria said, 'I found the punctuation homework easy to complete.'

b 'Would you like to come to my place to watch the Grand Final?' Tan asked Caleb.

c 'When will your Australian tour begin?' the reporter asked Kylie Minogue.

d 'Anzac Day was often identified with Gallipoli and not so much with the Western Front,' noted the History teacher.

e The Hollywood producer told the reporter, 'My film has likeable characters.'

Name: | Due date: | Guardian signature:

REVISION TEST 6

The two passages in this test are from John Branfield's novel *Nancekuke*. The novel tells the story of Helen's mission to discover the truth about her father's mysterious death at a chemical weapons research station. In the process, Helen learns about herself and uncovers a shocking truth.

1 Read the extract below. The letters in square brackets match the questions below. Answer each question.

On the following morning was the first of the examinations. Helen [**a**] did not feel too bothered about it, as they started with English Language [**b**]. There was nothing to revise, [**c**] and she would probably have passed it in the summer if she had not been absent.

At nine o'clock [**d**] she was outside the examination room, one of a small group shivering partly with cold and partly with nervousness. At least this time it was not held in the gym, filled with row upon row of desks. Each girl clutched a little plastic bag of pens and pencils.

They [**e**] shuffled their feet and hugged their arms in tight to keep warm. [**f**] A teacher arrived, and they went inside to find their places with their numbers. Helen arranged her things on the desk, put a heading on the answer paper and listened to the instructions as they were read. [**g**] The question papers were handed out in silence. The only sounds were the rustling of paper and the teacher's [**h**] footsteps.

She had not felt particularly anxious before, [**i**] but now her heart was pounding.

'Open your paper and begin,' [**j**] said the teacher.

Branfield, J 1988, *Nancekuke*, Gryphon Books, London, p. 103.

a Why has a capital letter been used? ______________________

b Why have capital letters been used? ______________________

c Why has a comma been used? ______________________

d Why has an apostrophe been used? ______________________

e Why has a capital letter been used? ______________________

f Why has a full stop been used? ______________________

g Why has a comma been used in the previous sentence? ______________________

h Why has an apostrophe been used? ______________________

i Why has a comma been used? ______________________

j Why have quotation marks been used? ______________________

c *Singing boisterously*, the hikers began their descent. ____________

d *Pushing his little wooden train* is Patrick's favourite game. ____________

e The wagon appeared *between the trees*. ____________

2 Underline the adjectival phrase in each of the following sentences.

a Patrick has a toy train made of wood.

b Madeleine is a young girl with determined views.

c The hockey sticks with the pink grips are mine.

d All performers with a serious commitment will improve their skills.

e Singing boisterously, the hikers began their descent.

3 Underline the adverbial phrase in each of the following sentences.

a The cricketers were not playing during the torrential rain.

b The scooter was purchased before Christmas.

c The young shopper walked in a dream.

d The wagon appeared between the trees.

e The performers were singing with enthusiasm.

4 Underline the noun phrase in each of the following sentences.

a Pushing his little wooden train is Patrick's favourite game.

b He does not like reading comics.

c I know how to cook doughnuts.

d Eating beetroot is something I try to avoid.

e Teasing his sister was Lee's favourite pastime.

TAKE IT FURTHER

1 Write whether the italicised phrases below are *noun* phrases, *adjectival* phrases or *adverbial* phrases.

a John sat at the kitchen table, *eating an ice-cream*. ____________

b *Eating an ice-cream* is a joy on a hot day. ____________

c The choir was singing *with enthusiasm*. ____________

d The hikers, *stumbling wearily*, could finally see their destination. ____________

e The hikers stumbled wearily *towards their destination*. ____________

2 Choose a phrase to complete each sentence and write whether the phrase is a *prepositional* or a *participial* phrase.

with obvious enthusiasm	slumped in his favourite armchair
reading graphic novels	written by Neil Gaiman

a ____________, he was reading his new graphic novel.
____

b He was reading his new graphic novel, ____________
____

c Unlike her brother, she does not like ____________
____

d He particularly enjoys graphic novels ____________
____

Name: | Due date: | Guardian signature:

31 DANGLING PHRASES

Phrases, clauses, sentences and paragraphs

Dangling phrases occur when a group of words is not attached to the correct noun or pronoun.

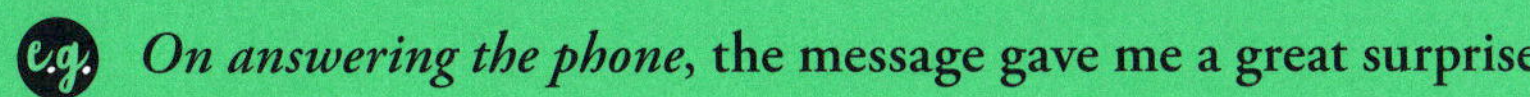

e.g. *On answering the phone*, the message gave me a great surprise.

A less confusing version would be:

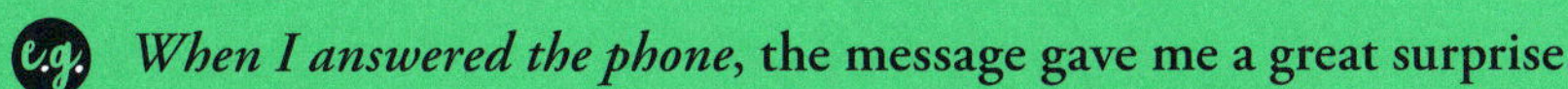

e.g. *When I answered the phone*, the message gave me a great surprise.

Make sure that your phrase relates clearly to the rest of the sentence, otherwise the location of the phrase makes the sentence ambiguous – that is, there are two possible interpretations.

e.g. *Through the window*, our friend saw the young man escape from the school across the street.

or

Our friend saw the young man escape *through the window* from the school across the street.

Clumsy positioning of participles confuses the reader. These sometimes referred to as dangling (or hanging) participles.

e.g. *Turning the corner*, the town hall came in sight.

Sometimes it is unclear who is responsible for the action.

e.g. After seeing the film, the book is a must-read.

This needs to be rewritten so that we know who is involved:

e.g. After seeing the film, Noah decided that the book was a must-read.

1 Rewrite the following sentences so that the meaning is clear.

a Furiously eating scraps in the pen, Adam eventually found his runaway pig.

b There was a cricket bat for sale from a coach with a pink grip.

c After singing a moving song, the crowd cheered the performer.

d Driving to the cinema, there was a lot of traffic on the road.

Misplacing a phrase can lead to unintended meanings.

e Being forced to close, the residents had to find another nursing home.

f Walking home from cricket, my nose got sunburnt.

g I have some muffins that Mum made in my school bag.

h While crossing on the pedestrian crossing, a car hit her.

TAKE IT FURTHER

1 In the passage below, underline the dangling phrases or hanging participles. Then rewrite the paragraph so that it is precise.

> Dancing on the balcony, a monkey climbed down the vine. Suddenly performing tricks, we regained our composure. Some of the party guests laughed at this unexpected performance. Soon after, we continued dancing and ignored the fun and games on the vine.

2 Rewrite the following passage so that the meaning is clear.

> Swimming alone, a shark spotted me in the deep. Panicking badly, the monster came for me without much warning. His dorsal fin was large and he was moving swiftly. Knowing it was probably curtains, the shark passed me by. After suffering so much fear, the predator disappeared without a trace.

Name: | Due date: | Guardian signature:

32 CLAUSES

Phrases, clauses, sentences and paragraphs

A **clause** is a group of words that contains a subject and a verb. There are two types of clauses:

→ main or independent clauses
→ subordinate or dependent clauses.

A **main or independent clause** usually makes complete sense on its own and expresses the main message of the sentence.

e.g. The campers returned at twilight.

There can be more than one main clause.

e.g. The national anthem ended *and* the crowd roared in anticipation of the ensuing contest. (two main clauses)

A **subordinate or dependent clause** is less important than the main clause in a sentence. It offers extra information but cannot stand alone. A subordinating conjunction, such as *if*, *that*, *when* or *because*, begins a subordinate clause. Clauses can be noun clauses, adjectival clauses or adverbial clauses.

e.g. The campers returned at twilight [main clause] because they had taken a wrong turn. [subordinate clause]

After the campers returned to camp, [subordinate clause] it began to rain. [main clause]

1 Identify whether each sentence below consists of:

→ one main clause
→ two main clauses
→ one main clause and one subordinate clause.
→ two main clauses and one subordinate clause

a I wanted to watch the horror film but it was getting late.

b The police officer chased the youths for several minutes.

c If you don't like my cooking you can make your own meal.

d I was thinking about my homework when it happened.

To identify a clause, work out the subject and verb relationship.

e I can't stand heavy-metal music.

f My favourite rock group is playing at the festival and the lead singer has promised to sign autographs for fans.

g He'll tell us about the match when he gets home.

h I'd love to have a dog but my father says that pets are too much work.

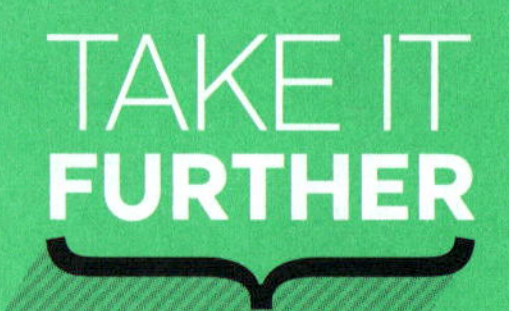

Just as phrases can be noun phrases, adjectival phrases and adverbial phrases, subordinate clauses can be noun clauses, adjectival clauses or adverbial clauses, depending on the function they perform in a sentence.

Each of the sentences below has only two clauses: a main clause and a subordinate clause. The subordinate clause is in italics. For each sentence, work out what type of clause the subordinate clause is: *noun* clause, *adjectival* clause or *adverbial* clause. Write noun, adjectival or adverbial in the space after each sentence.

Hint: the sentences are divided into three groups. In each group of three, there is one clause of each type.

a i I know *what you did last summer.* ________________

ii Last summer, *which seems so long ago now,* was a nightmare. ________________

iii *When I remember last summer,* the nightmares return. ________________

b i I, *who had implicit trust in you,* was terribly betrayed. ________________

ii I did not expect *that you would betray me.* ________________

iii *Because I trusted you implicitly,* your betrayal was a terrible shock. ________________

c i *After she had worked so hard,* her parents expected her to succeed. ________________

ii Her parents, *who had seen her work so hard,* expected her to succeed. ________________

iii Her parents hoped *that her hard work would be rewarded.* ________________

d i The committee reported *that the research had produced contradictory results.* ________________

ii The research, *which had produced contradictory results,* was outlined in the committee's report. ________________

iii *If the research results are contradictory,* more work will need to be done. ________________

Name: | Due date: | Guardian signature:

33 EMBEDDED CLAUSES

Phrases, clauses, sentences and paragraphs

Sometimes the subordinate clause is embedded inside another clause.

 The campers, who had been on a long hike, were drenched to the skin.

The campers were drenched to the skin is the main or independent clause; *who had been on a long hike* is a subordinate or dependent clause embedded within the main clause.

Embedded clauses, such as *who had been on a long hike*, extend the noun phrase, telling us more about the noun. For this reason, they are called adjectival clauses.

Here are some other examples:

 The rain, which had been expected all afternoon, was very heavy.
They were eager to reach their cabins, which would be warm and cosy.

Not all embedded clauses are adjectival clauses. It is quite common for adverbial clauses to be placed within other clauses, as in the following examples:

 Although, when he arrived home, Joe joked about the incident at school, he was obviously upset.

Joe joked about the incident at school is the main clause. *Although he was obviously upset* is a subordinate clause. *When he arrived home* is a subordinate clause embedded within another subordinate clause.

 I should like to take a holiday but, until I complete this assignment, I can't get away.

Here there are two main clauses: *I should like to take a holiday* and *but I can't get away. Until I complete this assignment* is a subordinate clause embedded within the second main clause.

Embedded clauses enable us to express complex ideas concisely.

1 Underline the embedded clauses in the following sentences. They are all adjectival clauses.

a The plane that they were watching suddenly exploded.
b The Queen, who was accompanied by her favourite corgi, waved at the people lining the street.
c Motorists who run red lights are endangering lives.
d The air show that had been so eagerly anticipated was called off.
e Red light cameras, which are installed at many intersections, have made motorists more cautious.
f The air show, which features some amazing planes from the Second World War, is held annually.
g Enthusiastic fans, who come from all over the country, love it.
h The local residents, who have to endure several days of noise, are less keen.

Embedded clauses can be used to extend noun groups

2 Underline the embedded clauses in the following sentences. They are all adverbial clauses.

- **a** If the team, when they came to practice last evening, had not put in a determined effort, the coach might have resigned.
- **b** The principal had made a decision, before the vandals confessed, to call the police.
- **c** I want to go to the cinema this evening but, unless you can come with me, I won't bother.
- **d** The position, if it had been advertised, would have attracted many applicants.
- **e** In a speech to the conference, after he had been awarded life membership, the president praised the committee members for their support.

TAKE IT FURTHER

1 Complete the following sentences by adding embedded clauses. Swap your work with a partner's and check each other's answers for complete clauses.

- **a** The team, which ______________________________ ______________ was hoping to win the tournament.
- **b** The team was captained by my friend Jake, who ______________________________ ______________________________
- **c** I held my breath as I watched the final moments, which ______________________________ ______________________________
- **d** It was a triumphant moment that ______________________________ ______________________________

2 Rewrite the following sentences according to the instructions.

- **a** My parents told me the news. I pretended not to hear. I was very anxious.
  Rewrite the three sentences as one sentence containing an embedded clause. Begin with the words: *Although, when . . .*
- **b** This tiger is a killer. When it was young, it was badly injured by hunters.
  Rewrite the two sentences as one sentence containing an embedded clause. Begin with the words: *This tiger is a killer because . . .*
- **c** You must finish your homework before you can go to the cinema with your friends. You must finish it before you go out.
  Rewrite the two sentences as one sentence containing an embedded clause. Begin with the words: *Unless, before . . .*

Name: | Due date: | Guardian signature:

34 SENTENCES

Phrases, clauses, sentences and paragraphs

You may have learnt in your first year at school that sentences begin with a capital letter and end with a full stop, a question mark or an exclamation mark, but errors with sentences are among the most common errors in student writing.

Most errors fall into the following two categories:

→ **run-on sentences**

These occur when sentences that should be kept separate are combined.

e.g. **Marius asked Gail to the party she accepted the invitation.**

The example above should be two sentences. They should have been written this way: 'Marius asked Gail to a party. She accepted the invitation.'

Sometimes, sensing that there is some kind of pause between the two sentences, writers put in a comma: 'Marius asked Gail to a party, she accepted the invitation.'

However, if they are separate sentences, each with its own finite verb ('asked' and 'accepted') they need a full stop (or question mark or exclamation mark, if appropriate).

→ **incomplete or fragmentary sentences.**

A sentence fragment is a set of words punctuated to look like a sentence but which is not a grammatically complete sentence. The following are phrases, not sentences, because they don't have a finite verb.

e.g. **Another day. Pretty boring.**

1 The following passage is an example of run-on sentences. Rewrite the passage, adding full stops and capital letters where they are needed.

Robert Cartwright was a Church of England clergyman and one of the first members of the clergy to work in the new colony of New South Wales he arrived in Sydney with his wife and six children in the convict ship *Anne* in 1810 his first appointment was to the Hawkesbury area where the town of Windsor had recently been established he transferred to the Liverpool district before the new church of St Matthew's at Windsor was completed that church was built by convict architect Francis Greenway and is acknowledged as one of the finest examples of his work

Sentence fragments are often used in colloquial speech but use them sparingly in writing.

2 The following passage contains a number of incomplete or fragmented sentences. Rewrite the passage, adding extra words and changing the punctuation if necessary.

Francis Greenway was an architect. Born in 1777 and died in 1837. Born in England in a family who had been builders for many years. In March 1812, he was convicted. Of forgery. The sentence for forgery in those days was the death penalty. Some death sentences were changed to sentences of transportation. Which was what happened in Greenway's case. He came to Australia on the convict ship *General Hewitt*. In February 1814.

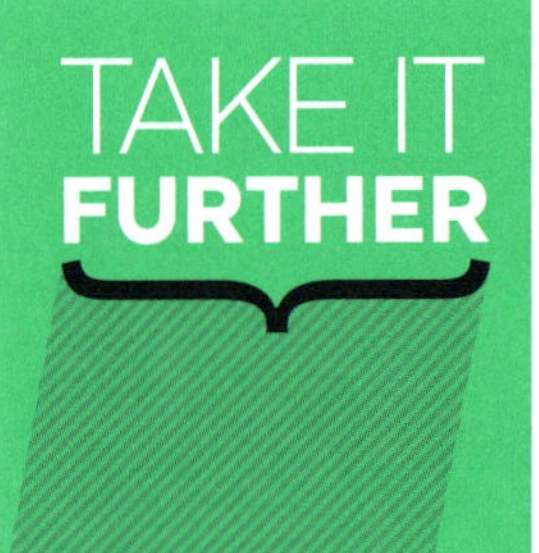

Some professional writers use sentence fragments cleverly for dramatic effect. This can be suitable in play scripts, poetry and novels.

Sentence fragments are also common in dialogue and speech.

 **'What do you think?'**

'Not much.'

In the above sentence fragment, the missing subject and verb are implied: '(I do) not (think) much.'

The dialogue below contains dramatic sentence fragments. Rewrite the dialogue in complete sentences. Remember to state the implied subject where appropriate.

 Silence!

What?

If they hear us above, we're in trouble.

Answer: We must be silent. I asked what the matter was. We will be in trouble if they hear us from above.

Can Mario kick the goal?

Precious time left.

Just one goal will do it.

Name: Due date: Guardian signature:

35 SENTENCE TYPES

Phrases, clauses, sentences and paragraphs

There are four types of sentences: simple, compound, complex and compound-complex.

→ A **simple sentence** has only a subject and predicate (see Unit 8). It consists of one main clause. The verb of the sentence belongs with the predicate. The predicate may also have one or more words that complete or clarify the meaning of the verb.

Sydney is a spectacular city. (subject: Sydney; predicate: is a spectacular city)

The sports complex was erected after a public campaign. (subject: The sports complex; predicate: was erected after a public campaign)

→ A **compound sentence** is made up of at least two main clauses joined by a conjunction or separated by a semicolon.

e.g. Sydney is a spectacular city and Melbourne is the most liveable.

The sports complex was erected after a public campaign; the old mansion nearby has been restored.

→ A **complex sentence** is made up of one main clause and one or more dependent or subordinate clauses. The main clause is the sentence itself in its basic form; the other clauses depend on it and add detail of less importance. In the following examples, the subordinate clauses are italicised.

e.g. They believed *that Santa Claus would deliver all the presents on the list.*

When I replied, he realised *who had left the telephone message.*

→ A **compound-complex sentence** is made up of at least two main clauses and one or more subordinate clauses.

e.g. They had made a long wish list and they believed that Santa Claus would deliver all the presents on the list.

The example above has two main clauses and one subordinate clause. The main clauses are 'They had made a long wish list' and 'they believed'. The subordinate clause is 'that Santa Claus would deliver all the presents on the list'.

1 Underline the main clause in each of the following complex sentences.

- **a** I followed them when I was walking up the narrow ravine.
- **b** The police officer yelled to the jaywalkers who were dodging the traffic.
- **c** When the waiter returned, he told us that steak had been removed from the menu.
- **d** They were puffing when they reached the summit.
- **e** After we had finished dinner, we decided that we would go to the cinema.
- **f** Although she had seen the film before, my sister decided to accompany us.
- **g** She said that she didn't mind seeing it again, because it was very funny.
- **h** Between the trees, the children found buried jewellery.
- **i** After the game, the girls celebrated their first footy win.
- **j** I discovered my passion at dancing classes.
- **k** Mother said that she mowed the lawn for Christmas Day.

Good writers select the type of sentences they use depending on their purpose.

2 Decide whether each sentence below is a *simple*, *compound*, *complex* or *compound-complex* sentence.

- **a** You need to heat some oil in a pan. ________________
- **b** When it begins to sizzle, you can add some chopped onions. ________________
- **c** You must watch the onions carefully, as you don't want them to burn. ________________
- **d** You can use brown onions, but I prefer red onions for this dish. ________________
- **e** While the onions are browning, you can slice the chicken into strips and you can measure out the spices that you will be adding. ________________
- **f** The grass is always greener on the other side. ________________
- **g** The grass is always greener on the other side but climbing the fence can be dangerous. ________________
- **h** While the grass is always greener on the other side, climbing the fence can be dangerous. ________________
- **i** While the grass is always greener on the other side, climbing the fence can be dangerous and it may be better to stay where you are. ________________

TAKE IT FURTHER

1 Combine the sentences below to form compound sentences.

- **a** We finished dinner. Then we went to the cinema. (Use *and*.)
- **b** We went to the cinema. My brother stayed at home. (Use *but*.)

2 Combine the sentences below to form complex sentences.

- **a** We finished dinner. We went to the cinema. (Use *before*.)
- **b** My brother stayed at home. He had urgent homework to do. (Use *because*.)
- **c** My sister came with us. She had already seen the film. (Use *who*.)

3 Underline one complex sentence and draw a wavy line under one compound-complex sentence in the following appeal for youth leadership.

> The future is now for youth. Now is the time for teenagers to make their plans and make a difference. Don't hold them back, Australia. They have lots of energy and will strive to make this country a closer community that future generations will remember with pride. Give them their opportunity to lead.

Name: | Due date: | Guardian signature:

36 COHESIVE TIES

Phrases, clauses, sentences and paragraphs

Cohesive ties are language features that we draw on to make sure that our communication is unified. They make connections between one part of a sentence and another, between sentences and between paragraphs.

For example, you might write a five-paragraph report. You might begin the second paragraph with *first*. Further paragraphs might begin with phrases such as *In the second place* or *A further example* … Your final paragraph might begin with *finally*. You have used **text connectives** (mainly adverbs or adverbial phrases) to give a logical sequence to your report.

We also use **lexical chains** or repetition of the same or related words to give unity to our writing. For example, you might write a report on surfing skills. You might repeat the word *surfing* several times, and you might use variations of the word such as *surfer* or *surfboard*. You will almost certainly use words that are closely associated with surfing, such as *water*, *beach*, *wave*, *wipeout* and *paddle*. These help hold the report together; they make connections and give a sense of unity to the writing. Similarly, if you wrote a persuasive piece about democracy you might use a number of synonyms, such as *freedom* and *liberty*, and possibly antonyms, such as *dictatorship* or *authoritarian regime*. Related words would include words such as *vote*, *voter*, *ballot box*, *universal franchise* and so on.

Two cohesive devices that we use naturally all the time are ellipsis and substitution. We say: *I like tennis, but not golf.* (We don't say: *I like tennis but I don't like golf.*) That's an example of ellipsis: we have left out some unnecessary words. We also say: *A professional tennis match like the one I saw last night is absolutely riveting!* We don't say: *A professional tennis match like the tennis match I saw last night is absolutely riveting!* That's an example of substitution: we have substituted the pronoun *one* for *tennis match*.

1 In the following passage, draw an arrow from the pronouns to the nouns they refer to.

> Juan is in Year 12. His favourite subject is physics and he intends to study science at university. His girlfriend, Cheryl, is in Year 11. She is a talented musician who plays in the school band. They like to meet for coffee after school.

2 In the following advertisement, underline all the words that belong to the main lexical chain.

> Escape this winter to a tropical paradise. Lounge on the balcony of your luxuriously appointed lodging, set in resort-style parkland. Indulge yourself with sumptuous meals in our deluxe waterfront restaurant. Pamper your senses with our delicious beauty therapies.

3 In the following paragraph about Arctic ice, underline all the words that form a lexical chain with *disappearing*.

> Arctic ice is disappearing at previously unseen rates. The melting has caused coastal ice in parts of Canada and Alaska to become quite brittle. That ice easily breaks away in large chunks and melts in the open ocean.

Cohesive ties make connections that unify our writing or speaking.

4 Remove unnecessary repetition in the following sentences by rewriting them, using ellipsis or substitution.

a I like playing AFL football but my brother prefers playing rugby.

b There are several different types of football. I chose AFL football.

c The team lists were laid out on a large table in the centre of the room. Every member of the club had to sign a list.

d The committee has held a number of fundraising activities during the year. The goal kick competition is a fundraising activity.

TAKE IT FURTHER

Text connectives such as *however, nevertheless, then, for example* and *on the other hand* are adverbs or adverbial phrases, not conjunctions. While they make connections between sentences, they do not join them. One of the most common errors in students' writing is to run on sentences, joining them with an adverb, when there should be two separate sentences.

e.g. I wanted to join the band however I failed the audition.

This is an example of a run-on sentence. It should be punctuated like this:

e.g. I wanted to join the band. However, I failed the audition.

Rewrite the following sentences, punctuating them correctly. In some cases, you might want to use a conjunction to join the sentences.

a Whip the cream then spoon it on top of the cake.

b I couldn't join the band consequently I had to choose a different recreational activity.

c James is a good AFL footballer, he's a better soccer player.

Name: | Due date: | Guardian signature:

37 BASIC PARAGRAPHS

Phrases, clauses, sentences and paragraphs

Paragraphs are the essential building blocks of essays and narratives. A paragraph:

- → begins with a **topic sentence** (or paragraph opener) that identifies the main idea or focus
- → contains several **explanatory sentences** that explain or illustrate the main idea outlined in the topic sentence and are logically organised
- → finishes with a **concluding sentence** that summarises the main idea.

Sentences within a paragraph are linked by cohesive ties such as:

- → pronouns that are used in place of a noun and refer back to that noun
- → conjunctions that link phrases and clauses together
- → connectives – mostly adverbs or adverbial phrases such as *however, consequently, on the other hand* and *firstly*
- → related words to make a lexical chain.

In print, the first word of a paragraph is usually indented. Paragraphs can vary in length: a basic guideline is from 25 to 250 words, or 1 to 10 sentences.

Read the example paragraph below. Identify and label the following paragraph features: indent, topic sentence, explanatory sentences, concluding sentence. Write your responses on and around the paragraph.

Bullying is intentional and repeated negative behaviour directed towards another person by one person or more people over time. It can be related to just about anything and can come in many forms. For example, bullying can include physical, verbal, social (like spreading rumours, excluding people, etc.) or sexual aggression, and it can be online or face-to-face. Cyber bullying is a form of bullying that uses technology (e.g. text messages, email and social networking sites such as Facebook, Instagram or YouTube), anonymously or not, to carry out the behaviour. Bullying can take place just about anywhere in many different forms.

'Bullying' Fact Sheet © headspace National Youth Mental Health Foundation Ltd, http://headspace.org.au/assets/Uploads/Resource-library/Family-and-friends/Bullying-FAF-web.pdf Accessed June 2016, reproduced with permission

All paragraphs need a topic sentence.

Match the notes in the box with the appropriate topic sentences below. Then organise the notes into logical order and write each paragraph in your workbook.

- → Includes Tasmania
- → Britain had an extensive convict problem due to economic and social changes which resulted in widespread poverty
- → Extensive deserts
- → Complex spiritual beliefs based on 'The Dreaming' when mythic beings created the world
- → Convicts used as labour to establish the Australian colony
- → Population of 21 261 000 lives mainly along coastal areas
- → Nomadic hunter-gatherers in small family clans
- → Newly independent American colonies refused to accept convicts
- → Covers a land area of 7 682 300 square kilometres
- → Arrived 40 000 to 60 000 years ago from Asian regions
- → The prison hulks on the Thames River were dangerously overcrowded
- → Great Dividing Range and Barrier Reef are significant geographical features

a 'Anthropologists believe that Indigenous Australians arrived during the last Ice Age.'

b 'Why did the British Government decide to send convicts to Botany Bay?'

c 'Australia is a significant continent in the Asia–Pacific region.'

Name: Due date: Guardian signature:

38 INFORMATIVE PARAGRAPHS

Phrases, clauses, sentences and paragraphs

Informative paragraphs explain and illustrate information on a particular topic, such as a person, place, process or event. These paragraphs include relevant definitions, facts and examples relating to the topic. The focus and coherence of the paragraph is achieved by organising the information into logical sequence; for example, chronological order, step-by-step order or sub-topics. Informative paragraphs are used in reports, biographies, nonfiction books, advertisements and reference books such as encyclopaedias and dictionaries. Generally, informative paragraphs incorporate conventional paragraph structure (topic sentence/paragraph opener, explanatory sentences and concluding sentence).

Read the following informative paragraph about witnessing bullying. Highlight a definition in green, an example in yellow and a fact in blue.

The Bystander.

Bullying is common, with up to 46.8% of Australian secondary school students reporting they have been bullied in some form over the past 12 months. Someone who sees or knows about bullying, but does nothing to stop it, is known as a bystander. A bystander plays a significant role in bullying. If you find yourself in this position, try not to accidentally support the bully by standing by and doing nothing, laughing at the person being bullied, or by "liking" nasty photos or posts online. It can help to tell the person being bullied that you are there for them, as they may be feeling very alone. If you see bullying and do not feel comfortable taking action yourself, report it to a trusted adult and let them know you want to be kept anonymous.

'Bullying' Fact Sheet © headspace National Youth Mental Health Foundation Ltd, http://headspace.org.au/assets/Uploads/Resource-library/Family-and-friends/Bullying-FAF-web.pdf Accessed June 2016, reproduced with permission

1 The following sentences inform about the process and effects of acid rain, but they are out of order. Rewrite them in the correct order, setting them out in paragraph form. Remember to indent your paragraph.

- → These pollutants may be transported long distances from their source in clouds or by wind conditions.
- → Acid rain has caused the poisoning of lakes and forests, erosion of structures, acid smog in cities and mutations in food crops and ecological systems.
- → Acid rain is a form of destructive air pollution that causes serious environmental damage.
- → Eventually, the acid pollutants fall to Earth through rain, snow or fog.
- → Acid rain occurs when industrial emissions such as sulphur and nitrogen combine with atmospheric moisture.

Informative paragraphs must be arranged in logical order.

List the features of a formal letter illustrated in the previous example. Begin with:

→ State your own name and address, including email address if appropriate.

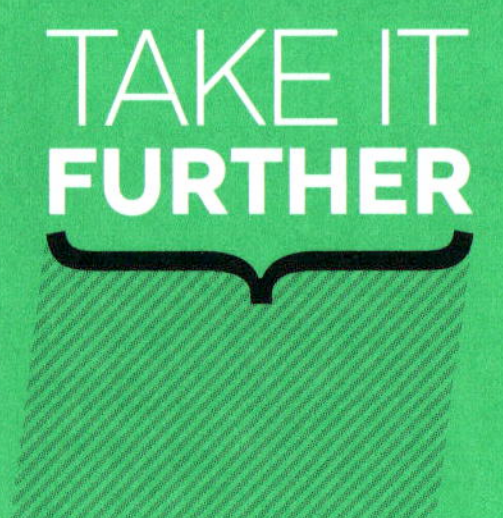

Email is used for important communications both inside and outside the workplace. Formal emails, including workplace emails, require the same attention to detail as formal letters. Use of emoticons and abbreviations is inappropriate. The subject line should be clear and provide sufficient information for the recipient to know why you are making contact. Emails are kept short as extra information should be contained in a separate attachment. On the other hand, because emails are concise and direct, it is possible to convey the wrong tone so re-read emails carefully before sending them. Always take sufficient time to reflect on your response to an email if you're the recipient and always observe the rules of netiquette.

1 Answer these questions about email procedure. Then discuss your answers with a partner.

a What is the difference between 'Reply' and 'Reply all'?

b What is the difference between 'Cc' and 'Bcc'?

2 What is wrong with this email? How would you correct the faults?

Hey miss

About that essay from the other day I don't think I can finish it cos I got training this afternoon and I have too much maths homework to do after that.

See ya

Damien, best English student ever – not!

Think carefully about whether everyone copied in needs to receive your reply or whether it is only relevant to the primary sender.

Name: Due date: Guardian signature:

40 WRITING AN ESSAY

Types of writing

The basic essay structure includes five paragraphs – one introductory paragraph, three body paragraphs and a conclusion. However, additional body paragraphs may be included, depending on the topic and the detail required.

→ The introductory paragraph identifies the subject of the essay. It defines key terms and gives a brief outline of the points that will be raised in the essay.

→ Body paragraphs expand on the subject. Each paragraph has a specific focus. This is signposted in a topic sentence. There are also explanatory sentences and a concluding sentence (see Unit 37). Body paragraphs include examples, facts and figures, definitions, key vocabulary, explanations and causes/effects. In order to achieve fluency, body paragraphs include appropriate cohesive ties (see Unit 36).

→ A concluding paragraph summarises the key ideas made about the subject.

In general, a five-paragraph essay is approximately 600 to 800 words in length.

In English, you are often required to write an essay outlining the changes and developments experienced by characters in novels. Select a character from the novel you are currently studying and complete the following essay outline by inserting appropriate responses. The following essay outline is a model only – you may alter words or phrases in the sentences to reflect your own style.

You could work in pairs to help each other improve your essays.

Essay topic: Outline the changes in the central character of a novel you have studied.

1 Introductory paragraph

→ Write one sentence outlining the essay topic in your own words.

→ Write one sentence summarising the text you are writing about.

→ Write one sentence briefly introducing and outlining the development of the central character.

e.g. In novels, characters experience major changes and developments. *Great Expectations* by Charles Dickens is set during the period after the Industrial Revolution in England and explores the changes in the main character, Pip, as a consequence of his ambitions. In the novel, Pip changes from an innocent boy to a selfish snob and finally to an honest and likeable young man.

An essay must have a clear introduction and a conclusion.

2 First body paragraph

Firstly, at the beginning of the novel, ______________________________ *(insert main character's name)* is ______________________ and ___________________________ *(insert two adjectives to describe the character's personality)*. A significant quote about ______________________ *(insert main character's name)* from the opening section is:

____

(insert a quote from the text – use quotation marks and give the page number in brackets).

This suggests that ______________________ *(insert main character's name)* ________________ ____ *(insert a comment about what the quote reveals about the main character).*

3 Second body paragraph

Following on, a major turning point for ______________________ *(insert main character's name)* is when ____ *(describe an incident where the main character changes)*. This shows that ______________________ *(insert main character's name)* ____

____ *(insert a comment about what the turning point reveals about the main character).*

4 Third body paragraph

Subsequently, by the end of the novel, ______________________ *(insert main character's name)* has changed, displaying the following qualities: ______________________ and ______________________ *(insert nouns describing the main character)*. This illustrates that ______________________ *(insert main character's name)* ____

____*(insert a comment about what the change reveals about the main character).*

5 Conclusion

On the whole, ______________________ *(insert main character's name)* changes throughout the novel. In overview, the main changes are: ____ ______________________ and ____ ____ *(briefly summarise two changes referred to in your essay).*

Swap your essay with another student's and review each other's work.

Name: | Due date: | Guardian signature:

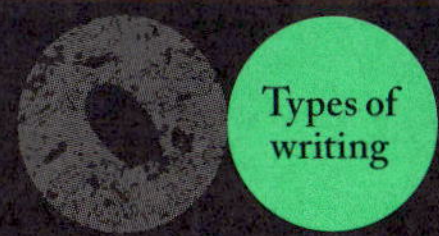

SPELLING FOCUS 3

1 Write the correct homophone in each space below.

a I ________________ ate the apple but it was not a ________________ experience. (holy/wholly)

b The ________________ gave his speech but the ________________ of his moral message was lost on many students. (principle/principal)

c I shouted myself ________________ at the game and I came home and ate like a ________________. (horse/hoarse)

d At the zoo, I liked looking at the cute ________________ cub even though its protective mother would ________________ her teeth at me. (bare/bear)

e My mischievous brother would not ________________ until he could ________________ my tablet from me. (wrest/rest)

f There was a ________________ in traffic so the driver released his hand ________________ quickly. (brake/break)

g Farmers ________________ their fields and embroiderers ________________ their fabric. (sew/sow)

h With their nimble ________________, the dancers achieved a great ________________ on stage in front of the Queen. (feat/feet)

i The cut on my ________________ has been washed and bandaged; it should ________________ nicely. (heal/heel)

2 In each of the following sentences an incorrect homophone has been used. Circle the incorrect word then write the correct spelling.

a Books and stationary will be on sale tomorrow at lunch time. ________________

b I am dreading my interview with the principle. ________________

c He asked me weather I was interested in joining the team. ________________

d The school councillor is the best person to talk to if you have a problem. ________________

e The cheque is in the male. ________________

f I don't want to miss my favourite soapie cereal. ________________

g They often have cheep DVDs for sale. ________________

h Your passport will be checked as you cross the boarder. ________________

3 These are harder. A spellchecker program would accept all the sentences below. However, each one contains a word that is misspelt. Underline the misspelt word then write the correct word.

- **a** I've been reluctant to brooch the subject with him. ________________
- **b** This tropical island is known for its barmy evenings. ________________
- **c** Hamlet was called to meet the troop of actors. ________________
- **d** You will need to be on your metal if you want to do well in the exam. ________________
- **e** Can you think of any way of lightning his load? ________________
- **f** The miners struck a load of precious metal. ________________
- **g** Some birds, including some types of miners, can imitate human speech. ____________
- **h** The bridle party assembled for photographs. ________________
- **i** Which coarse is your brother doing at university? ________________
- **j** This hilly forested country is ideal for gorilla warfare. ________________

4 Write a sentence showing how each word in the pairs below is used. Work with a partner to check your work.

a farther – father

____

____

b hire – higher

____

____

c manor – manner

____

____

d night – knight

____

____

e sheer – shear

____

____

f weak – week

____

____

5 The most common misspellings in the English language occur in the most common words. Underline the correct spelling in each bracketed pair below.

a (Who's / Whose) (you're / your) best friend?

b (Theirs / There's) no doubt that (your / you're) reading has improved greatly.

c (Theirs / There's) no question that they were told to put (they're / their /there) books over (they're / their / there) on the table.

d (Who's / Whose) left this book behind?

e (Who's / Whose) book is this?

f (It's / Its) easy to see that (your / you're) making more effort.

g (There / They're) close friends.

h (They're / Their) coming to the party tonight.

i The cat was licking (its / it's) paw.

j (You're / Your) no friend of mine.

k (Its / It's) good to be on the winning side.

l Can you give me (they're / their) number?

m What's (you're / your) favourite?

6 **a** Explain in writing the difference between *you're* and *your*.

b Explain in writing the difference between *it's* and *its*.

c Explain in writing the difference between *they're* and *their*.

d Explain in writing the difference between *who's* and *whose*.

7 Here are the some important words for the metalanguage of English – the words you need when talking and writing about English. In each case, one, two, three or four letters have been left out. Rewrite the words, adding the missing letters.

a cl_ _se ______________

b gramm_r ______________

c particip_ _ ______________

d a_ _iteration ______________

e sp_ _ch ______________

f sp_ _ker ______________

g meta_ _or ______________

h simil_ ______________

i gra_ _atical ______________

j aux_ _ _ary ______________

k adverb_ _l ______________

l met_language ______________

m playwri_ _t ______________

n r_ythm ______________

o r_yme ______________

p thes_ _rus ______________

q repet_ _ _ _n ______________

r tra_edy ______________

8 Guess the words from the following clues. They all have something to do with school and they can be tricky to spell. If you are unsure of the spelling of your guess, check a dictionary.

a This noun of nine letters begins with a *p*, ends with *l* and is frequently confused with its homophone. It can also be used as an adjective meaning 'main' or 'chief.' ______________

b This noun is also frequently confused with its homophone, which refers to an elected local government representative. Beginning with *c*, it has 10 letters and refers to a trained specialist who has a range of roles to play, including advising students who have personal problems or learning difficulties. ______________

c This nine-letter noun refers to an important person who helps keep the school running, from the office rather than the classroom. It begins with the letters *sec*. ______________

d This adjective, beginning with *s*, has nine letters. Of the three levels of education, this is the middle one. ______________

e This begins with the word *question* because it contains lots of them. You might need to prepare one of these if you are going to interview people for research in the social sciences. It has 13 letters. ______________

f You might be the best writer in the class but unless you can make one of these your ability to communicate your ideas to others is limited. It has six letters, beginning with *sp*. ______________

g This begins with an *a* and ends with a popular noun suffix. It has 10 letters in all. This is something that has to be handed in. ______________

h Most canteens have one of these. It begins with the letter *q* and all four of the other letters are vowels. ______________

Name:

Due date:

Guardian signature:

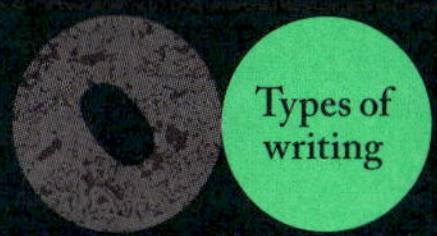

REVISION TEST 8

1 Answer the following questions using this sentence: 'A brown fox jumped lazily over the dog and cat'.

a Name the three nouns. ____________________

b Name the verb. ____________________

c Name the adjective. ____________________

d Name the adverb. ____________________

e Name the indefinite article. ____________________

f Name the definite article. ____________________

g Name the preposition. ____________________

h Name the conjunction. ____________________

2 Fill in the gaps in the following table of word families.

	Noun	Verb	Adjective	Adverb
a	admiration			
b				bitterly
c		care		
d			creative	
e		criticise		
f	depth			
g			foolish	
h				inventively
i	moisture			
j		reveal		

3 Provide a word with a prefix for each definition below. The part of speech is provided.

a bring goods into the country (verb) ______________________________

b not ordinary (adjective) ______________________________

c an error (noun) ______________________________

d an extremely wealthy person (noun) ______________________________

e lacking loyalty (adjective) ______________________________

4 Provide a word with a suffix for each definition below. The part of speech and suffix are provided.

a abundant (adjective, *-ful*) ______________________

b without restraint (adverb, *-ly*) ______________________

c very attractive (adjective, *-ful*) ______________________

d playing in the spirit of the game (noun, *-ship*) ______________________

e talking too much (adjective, *-ative*) ______________________

5 Write the correct prefix to form antonyms of the following words. Choose from *mis–, il–, mal–, im–*.

a ________moderate

b ________licit

c ________mortal

d ________manage

e ________nourished

f ________literate

g ________passable

h ________moral

i ________adventure

j ________logical

k ________function

l ________match

6 What type of sentence is each of the following – *simple, compound, complex* or *compound-complex*?

a Gorillas live in the tropical forests. ______________________

b If a gorilla beats its chest, it is angry. ______________________

c When they are angry, they beat their chests. ______________________

d Gorillas, which are endangered, live in the tropical forests. ______________________

e Gorillas are herbivores and are the largest primates on Earth today. ______________________

f Gorillas, which live in the tropical forests, are herbivores and they are also the largest primates on Earth today. ______________________

g Gorillas are also bred in captivity. ______________________

7 Refer to exercise 6 and answer the following questions.

a How many clauses are there in question **f**? ______________________

b Find the subordinate clause in question **c**. ______________________

c Find the subordinating conjunction in question **b**. ______________________

d What is the main clause in question **d**? ______________________

e Which punctuation mark is used to indicate clauses? ______________________

8 Rewrite the following passage in four separate sentences.

Gorillas live in the tropical forests they climb trees in search of food when they are angry they beat their chest a single blow from a gorilla's hand can kill a human

9 Rewrite the following passage in five separate sentences.

Chimpanzees belong to the ape family most chimpanzees live in West and Central Africa they are the closest living relatives to humans modern research has shown that chimpanzees can make and use tools they are also clever problem solvers

10 Underline the incorrect spelling in the following young readers' responses to *Harry Potter and the Chamber of Secrets*. Rewrite the words, spelling them correctly.

Katie, wearing big, round spectacles, said: 'I couldn't beleive how brave and glamourous and colorful the main character is, standing up to bullys and giant spiders!'

Gino, in a witch's hat, replied: 'Yes, but what I liked was the magic. And he's kind of like me. He's not a marrionette or a credullous monkey!' He's my size and Hermione is like my sister. She's not as smart as she thinks!'

11 Underline the words spelt incorrectly in the following passage and rewrite them, using correct spelling.

Whatever the fans of the books say, they are agreed that the intreguing play of opposites, the dark conection between young heros having to make decisions in difficult circumstances, to percieve good or decieve a bully, revenge something hurtful or devize something creative – all this makes the story colorful and eagerly sort after in librarys and bookstores.

12 Underline the words spelt incorrectly in the following review of a popular film. Rewrite the words, spelling them correctly.

> This beautifull and moveing film explores the universall themes of love and rejection, gender rolls and the surch for identity in the world. The performances are sintillating in a film that transends language and culture from the fishing sures to the depths of the see. The caracters are acountable for their decisions and a tribal girl makes her destany. This poynant film captures your sole, stirrs your senses, and mixes education and entertainment, offereing something special for everyone.

---

13 Read the following passage carefully and complete the exercises that follow.

> Passion. Live it. We often hear today the importance of having a passion for what we like to do. Go for it! Passion can give you that push to achieve difficult challenges. Sitting in the comfort zone, opportunities can pass you by. Passion is a strong emotion or drive to do something that we all can feel but not all people bother to nurture and then may start blaming others for their own lack of progress or success, which is not a responsible attitude to life. Seize the day. Aware. Alert. Seek.
>
> Passionate people are confident and resilient. The stuff of dreams, passion is vital.

Find an example of each of the following in the passage above and write it in the spaces provided.

a A fragmentary sentence

---

b A sentence that is much too long

---

c A dangling or hanging participle

---

d An exclamation

---

14 In your notebook, write a paragraph of 250 words on one of the following topics:

→ What are the benefits of a part-time job for teenagers?

→ Explain the ways in which teenagers can protect themselves in online environments.

→ Describe your ideal vision of the future world.